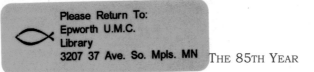

W9-ATY-966

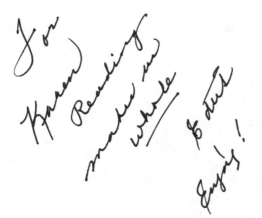

For
Karen)
Reading
marked me
whole
to start
Enjoy!

The 85th YEAR

by

Edith Mucke

Edith Mucke
7 October 2001

NORTH STAR PRESS OF ST. CLOUD, INC.

Library of Congress Cataloging-in-Publication Data

Mucke, Edith, 1914-
    The 85th year / by Edith Mucke.
        p. cm.
    ISBN 0-87839-167-3 (alk. paper)
    1. Mucke, Edith, 1914- 2. Aged women—
Minnesota—Minneapolis—Biography. 3.
Minneapolis (Minn.)—Biography. I. Title: Eighty-
fifth year. II. Title.

CT275.M6768 A3 2001
977.6′579053′092--dc21
[B]   2001040199

Front and back cover photos of
scenes at Lake of the Isles
by Alec Soth

Printed in the United States of America by Versa
Press, Inc., East Peoria, Illinois.

Published by
North Star Press of St. Cloud, Inc.
P.O. Box 451
St. Cloud, Minnesota 56302

First Edition

Dedication

This book is dedicated to
residents and staff of Kenwood Isles,
to the memory of my husband,
Paul Mucke (1903 to 1990),
my parents,
Bessie Nelson Johnson (1879 to 1953),
for my daughters,
Catherine Elizabeth and Jane Lynn,
and for all the readers who know that to live a long
and happy life you must grow older every year.

Acknowledgments

I would like to thank Paulette Alden, author and teacher, whose encouragement and professional critiquing inspired me and fueled my passion for writing and sharing my struggles with old age.

I am grateful to Kathy Vessells, Sabina Zimering, Toni McNaron, and all the women in my Noname Reading Group who listened to me read and offered suggestions.

I am especially grateful to Lucy Bowron, who kept gently nudging me. "Go write!" she said. "Remember you are a legend."

I am grateful to my daughter Cathy, who read, critiqued and jogged my memory, and to Jane, who computerized the entire manuscript. Without their encouragement and faith in my work, this manuscript would never have been completed.

I thank the friendships that make my life what it is. Old longtime friends Alice Newman, Vera Schletzer, Lou Christenson—who make up my bridge foursome—keep me humble and grounded; young friends Sherry Vaughan, Su Phenix, Liza Lawrence, and Mary Ellis, who feel like family and bring out the best in me. I thank Betty Clarke and Betty Porteous, who spent long hours in talk with me.

Foreword

A few years ago I complimented my friend Edith Mucke on her beautiful new coat. Somewhat sheepishly, she confessed that she had fallen in love with it and maybe had paid too much. But she had come to justify the expense.

"I decided that I could afford it," she explained, "if I never buy popcorn again at movie theaters."

That's Edith. Always thinking. Even when she leaves a message on my telephone answering machine, she has interesting stories to relate and observations to make. Sometimes her parting statement is, "This is Edith." As if it could be anyone else.

Edith Mucke came into my life when she was still in her seventies and has stuck in my heart.

It was June of 1994. She was about to turn eighty. More important, she was about to have her first book published. (Already she was referring to *Beginning in Triumph* as her first. *The 85th Year*, seven years later, is her second.)

Somehow I drew the assignment as a *Star Tribune* reporter to write about Edith and her book. We sat at her kitchen table with cups of coffee, and she told me her life story. Like the book, she was warm but honest. Her tale was unglossed. The ups, the downs—it was all there. I liked her, not *because of* her age or *in spite of* her age. I just liked her.

On her eightieth birthday—the release date for her book—I got to watch her in full form. She was ecstatic at the publication party that her niece threw for her. I said to Edith, "You have more people lined up for your autograph than Garrison Keillor gets." Her editor responded with a laugh, "He's not eighty."

Most of the well-wishers were women, some of whom had continued their education because of Edith. She had been the director of the University of Minnesota's Continuing Education for Women program. Besides that, she's always subtly pushing women—lots of us—to push ourselves.

When people that day told Edith she was an inspiration, she responded, "I'm walking on air. You know, the world has a preconceived notion of what it is to be eighty. This is what it is! I'm not in a walker, I'm not sick, I'm signing my book. I love this day."

*   *   *

She loves every day.

When her doctor recommended exercise, she not only signed up at the YWCA but also hired a personal trainer, a really handsome young man named Michael. (She does have good taste.) Pretty soon, she was walking around the Y track with two-pound weights and working out on exercise machines.

"I'm an old woman, and I don't mind," she told me, "but I don't want to be a little old lady. I don't want to be fragile. I hate the idea of being fragile."

So convincing was she about her exercise program that I wrote about it for the newspaper. She wanted me to include—and I did—that she had her share of physical problems: a mastectomy twenty years before, a small stroke in 1992, a bad car crash the next year. She gets peeved at people who say, "Oh, Edith, you're so lucky. Your life has been so easy." It's not all luck, she says. I know from watching: she works hard at making the most of life.

Edith at eighty.

Offsetting her problems have been a combination of physical and mental factors for which she thanks the loving universe. She was raised a Christian Scientist, which trained her in a positive outlook. (She left the faith and is a regular at Plymouth Congregational Church in Minneapolis.) She started taking hormones at age thirty-nine and believes they've helped keep her young.

She eats right, she entertains splendidly, she reads widely, she walks, she sits on park benches and contemplates, she collects friends, she knows her friends' friends, she enjoys a glass or two of wine, she loves and bolsters up family members, she loves to laugh, she listens.

She pays attention.

And she writes movingly. We'd be wise to pay attention too.

But, please, don't consider *The 85th Year* a prescription on how to age gracefully. That's the last thing Edith wants. She's never preachy, never arrogant enough to think, "It worked for me, and it can work for you."

Consider her book the well-told story of one individual blessed with good genes and a good attitude. Not everyone can be as vital, as open to new experiences, as accepting of the infirmities that come with age, as appreciative of each day as Edith.

As she told me recently (days before her eighty-seventh birthday), "It's very hard for me to be an old woman because I've never been one before. I'm still learning how. This is not a how-to book. I just want to tell people it's fine to be this age."

I'm thirty-two years behind her, and I feel fortunate to have the spirit of Edith living on these pages.

Peg Meier
Minneapolis, Minnesota
June 2001

Contents

I find my feet have further goals
I smile upon the aims
That felt so ample yesterday—
Today's have vaster claims.
I do not doubt the self I was
Was competent to me;
But something awkward in the fit—
Proves that outgrown I see.

—Emily Dickinson

For all that has been, thanks.
For all that is to be, yes.

—Dag Hammarskjöld
Secretary General, 1953 to 1961

Prologue

Boy on a Bench

May 1999

It is a late Sunday afternoon in May, a couple of hours before dinner time. Lured by the weather, I walk to the lake. "The lake" is Lake of the Isles in Minneapolis, a lake I consider a part of my front lawn. Sunday, family day. Children's voices, lovers strolling hand in hand. A day as warm as July or August in Minnesota. I fill my lungs with the soft air, know the luxury of the summer-like breeze on my skin. I remind myself of the joys of old age; no need to walk as fast as I can, no need to consult my watch, no power walk for me, I will saunter awhile, find a bench.

I do saunter. I love being alone, love the silence, love the unhurried clouds in the sky, their reflection in the water. Disturbed by nothing, I watch the stately ducks and geese gliding in all their majesty. I saunter on and then, unmindful of my friend Lucy's opinion that an old woman talking to herself, "muttering," seems shameful and humiliating, I begin reciting the wonderful lines of Wu Men, a twelfth century poet,

> Ten thousand flowers in spring
> the moon in autumn
> A cool breeze in summer
> Snow in winter
> if your mind is not clouded by unnecessary things,
> this is the best season of your life.

Soon, I give my body to a bench. In a few minutes, a young man approaches. "Name's Michael Roberts," he says extending his hand, "Mind if I join you? I need to get away from stuff and things."

"I'm Edith Mucke," I say, acknowledging the introduction. Of course I am happy to have him join me. Depositing sacks of corn and oats beside my bench, he walks to the shore. There are many geese, those large long-necked Canada geese whose excrement we natives deplore, birds that are a great attraction for not only children but adults who remember skipping stones and playing in the water.

I watch him. Michael is a very unfair gift giver, discriminating in lordly fashion against the geese, wanting to feed the ducks and especially the very young ones. I am peaceful, no need to pay attention to a non-functioning mind, enjoying "the best season of my life." When Michael empties the first bag, he returns to our bench.

In the shortest of possible times, he gives me a short biography: he's tired, really "sick and tired" of being a caregiver, and he has just buried his father in Michigan. He goes on with fervor—he's been lured here by a female. "You females," he says, "have a way of leading, making us males follow." He begins to tell me about his childhood. (Everyone has a story; some are more interesting than others. Much depends on the storyteller.) Now, here is what I know about this handsome young man, a *darling* young man, who will next week celebrate his fortieth birthday: Dysfunctional family with a father who drank too much, a mother who was depressed too much of the time. He took care of the younger kids, worked his way through the University of Michigan, went to grad school in Madison, where he met the young woman he is staying with right now. They have been together ten years, broken up, off and on, many times. He is Catholic. He is just not into all this working and striving and wanting a house in the suburbs and fancy cars. All *he* wants is a child, one child, one house, a roof over his head, and four walls. All these friends—people he knows, striving and slaving for dollars. And then their lives are gone, and they are old and what do they have? He wants to travel, has just been to Costa Rica, and I should go see the *divine place*. I tell him I have just come from the Wisconsin countryside, and I found the rolling green hills, the cows in green pastures, the pristine farms all *divine*. What's wonderful about Minneapolis? He wonders if it is better than Madison and thinks he'd vote for Madison.

When I tell him I'm about to turn eighty-five, he wonders what it is really like to be eighty-five. He says he wants to live a very long time because he wants to find out what it would be like. He thinks it would be fun to see how things turn out. "I want to live to be as old as you are. I want to know what it is like to be eighty-five years old." He talks more about the world and how the wrong-thinking people have all the power. Can't face the over-population problem. Again, he wants a child. *One* child. Importance of continuity. When I ask him how he plans to earn the money to travel and have the one house and the child, he says his choice would be to work as a salesman. I assure him that I can see he'd have no problem with his good looks, his charm, his winning per-sonality. Is it coming through that I am falling in love with him? There is indeed a wonderful freedom in being almost eighty-five years old. I am free to fall in love with anyone I choose! I am watching his mouth. Why do I always watch mouths instead of eyes that the authors of novels describe so eloquently? His hair is light, he is a blond. He is widely read. We have loved many of the same books. We talk fast and loud; we talk in the most convincing tones—platitudes and nonsense. Agreements and arguments.

Finally, he stands, faces the lake, turns to me and says the reason he is so depressed and ambivalent and frustrated is because he knows this should be the best time of his life and it really isn't—"I'm not enjoying it." Then he turns toward the lake again, and I hear him say, "If the mind is not cloud-ed by unnecessary things, this is the best season of my life."

When I hear him say that, I continue, "Ten thousand

flowers in spring, the moon in autumn." Now it is his turn to be surprised. He turns around, faces me, and together we say, "a cool breeze in summer, snow in winter. If your mind isn't clouded with unnecessary things, this is the best season of your life." We laugh, knowing that we are indeed kindred souls.

Twilight is playing with the colors on the water. I make a move, suggesting I must be going. He says, "I have to go too. She'll be mad." Then, abruptly, and with no leading up to his question, he asks, "What with all your wisdom is most important?" I say, "To forgive." Holding hands, we walk up the hill together, he to return to the woman who "might be mad." I, to the rest of my life, the best season of my life—to ponder what it's really like to be eighty-five—and to wonder, too, if "to forgive" was the right answer.

Chapter One

Pen in Hand

*June—85⁰—At my typewriter. Early morning, already hot and sticky. Out my window, people on Humboldt Ave. in shorts.
Ready to write.*

Pen in hand. I love those words. Makes me think of Samuel Johnson or Pepys and his journals or the first Japanese geishas who kept pillow books. Or I might think of Shakespeare and the prophets but that's stretching a bit too much. I wish I could write like Colette or Virginia Woolf or Michael Cunningham who has written, in shimmering prose, *The Hours*, a book I've been reading. Yesterday, my birthday, I was eighty-five years old. Spring has raced by, or have I raced through it? So today I am beginning my eighty-fifth year. That young man on the park bench said he'd like to live to be old so he'd know what it is like. I want to know what it's really like, too. The best way for me to know what being eighty-five really IS, is to push stuff around in this dusty attic of my mind and see if I can make room for words about being eighty-five—all the stuff piled up there, probably lots of cobwebs.

Birthdays. My birthday. SPAGHETTI AND TOMATOES WITH BACON. My mother has been dead for almost fifty years. The memory of the last birthday party she had for me when I was thirty-seven is as vivid as the memory of the birthday I had yesterday. Yellowish spaghetti all mixed up and

1

cooked with canned tomatoes and tiny pieces of brown fried bacon. That's what Mama served my friends and cousins and me. We were in the deliciously cool recreation room of the house on Thomas Avenue, close to the Lake Harriet tennis courts, where they moved when they sold the General Store in Triumph. It was a hot day.

Birthdays on the 14th of June were always hot or cold. That's Minnesota weather, unpredictable. Once when I was young it was so cold on my birthday, Mama made a soft coal fire in the kitchen stove and baked me a blueberry pie.

Today the scene outside the bay window is green on green, a verdant landscape framing flowers pink and yellow. I can't see the lake, but I know it's beyond all that green, and above, a clear blue sky.

I love remembering, thinking about my mother. My mother and her love for me. My comfort and security in her presence are with me now. I look at the small rocker in my bedroom, the rocker that was in *her* bedroom, the rocker in which she nursed my sister Ruth and me.

I'm thinking about my birthday, and I'm thinking about writing. I really do wish I could write like Colette, Virginia Woolf, or Michael Cunningham. But now I must stop wishing and stop comparing. Try to heed the admonitions of a Jon Kabat Zinn tape: "Try not to indulge in the common tendency to wish things were different from how they are." One of the things about being eighty-five is that I have learned how to use that advice which seems sensible, advice that works for me.

Different from thinking about Colette or Woolf, my mind turns to other scenes. My old giant of a grandfather. He sits at a round oak table in the kitchen. Grandmother hovers over a pot roast on the stove. They are in the St. Louis Park house where they lived out their last days. In front of För (as we called my grandfather) is a tablet of blank paper, and he drives a sturdy thumb nail across the edge of the ruler causing indentations that make lines. The lines now ready for his carefully formed letters of elegant script, he writes letters to

2

relatives in Sweden. He also writes weekly letters to his three married daughters living in small towns in Minnesota.

My mother continued the tradition. I see her sitting at our dining room table with the Jacobean legs, writing to Ruth and me on Sunday nights. I continued the practice, writing to my daughter Jane every week after she left for college in that glorious time before e-mail and fax communications and cheap telephone connections. You could put a *letter* under your pillow or carry it around in your purse. You could tie a ribbon around a pack of letters.

I'm still thinking about writing and my birthdays and now Gonzagas pops on the scene. Last year, I accepted my grandson Marc's invitation to come to Reno on June 14th to spend the weekend of my eighty-fourth birthday with him. I blew out the candles for my eighty-fourth birthday on a very large cake at the Hilton Hotel. We celebrated my birthday, his purchase of a house, and a big promotion for him at the Hilton. I admired his house, slept in his guest room, visited his spacious new office, met his secretary, enjoyed the view from the outside windows of the office and an extravagant musical production on a stage big enough to house an airplane. But that was only the beginning of my birthday celebration.

Gonzagas is part of this memory because it's closely connected to the theme of writing whirling about in my head. My friend Joanne was planning to buy me a lobster dinner in Boston after I returned from Reno. True, it would be two weeks late but at this age, who counts?

This friend, Joanne Zimmer, who lives in Denver and is forty years younger than I am, invited me to attend a ten-day retreat with her at Gonzagas, in Gloucester, Massachusetts. She'd been there the previous summer. Descriptions of the beautiful landscapes, the ocean, the wonder of living in silence as well as being with Joanne for that time proved irresistible. And then there was that lobster dinner in Boston for my birthday present. I dreamed of long walks in the woods, seeing a new-to-me part of the country, thinking about myself

and my life and where I was. Where was I going? All these
additional years I'd been given, a gift of so much extra life.
My friends, my literature classes, my bridge foursome, my
book club, my time at the Y, movies—crowded hours and
days. But was all this right for me? Would I prefer more structure? Did I lack a focus? No desire to *waste* time. Was I *using*
it the best way possible? I had no prescribed notion of what I
expected to get from Gonzagas. I looked forward to our time
in Boston, the haute cuisine dinner, talk over our wine, no
curfew . . . I was eighty-four years old, and in another year I
would be eighty-five!

The first surprise was that Northwest Airlines aborted
the lobster dinner by changing my flight plans. An hour
before I left Minneapolis, they cancelled the plane I was to
take to Detroit. When I arrived in Detroit, the plane I was to
take to Boston was two hours late. Instead of a 6:00 arrival in
Boston, I reached our chosen hotel after midnight to find
Joanne had gone to bed. She got up and presented me a bot-
tle of Scotch she had brought to celebrate my arrival —"if you
ever arrive," she said. We opened the Scotch, talked until we
were very tired and looked forward to the next day.

Birthday brunch at the Longpiers Hotel the next
morning was elegant. White linen, sparkling glasses, silver
chafing dishes, crystal chandeliers. Buffet tables boasting
small mountains of fruit, shrimp, lobster and chicken salads,
roast chicken, lamb and beef roasts, hashed brown potatoes,
sausages, crepes with blueberry sauce, eclairs, champagne. A
banquet I enjoyed but no more than spaghetti and tomatoes.

While standing in front of the hotel, waiting for our
transportation, Joanne told me about Nancy, who was driving us to the retreat.

"Nancy," she said, "will be my spiritual counselor during these days. You also will have a spiritual counselor for one
hour each day. Nancy is authentic New England. You'll like
her. She writes poetry and has done work in liturgical dance.
I think of her as one of my best friends."

I was eager to meet Nancy. I knew she was a nun.

4

Nothing prepared me for what stepped out of her car when she arrived: blonde, small, with very short cropped hair, an athletic body—a dancer's body—wearing short khaki shorts and white T-shirt. With the strength of a longshoreman, she tossed our bags and got us into her car.

"My plan," announced Nancy, "is to drive you through the most scenic part of Cape Ann, around the island, then take you to lunch before you settle in."

And she did.

"Cape Ann," she said, is often called "the other cape" to distinguish it from better known Cape Cod, is literally an island, the Atlantic on three sides. The fourth side has a river of salt water that flows into Niles Pond, across the road from Gonzagas Eastern Point Retreat House." In her lovely soft but clear voice sounding oh so New England, Nancy gave us some of the history of Cape Ann. Settled in 1623, Cape Ann was a fishing center, but in the last two centuries its other lifeblood has been granite. Gloucester, once one of the busiest fishing ports in the country, resembles Edward Hopper paintings.

This drive was a great gift to Joanne and me. Even though it was familiar to Joanne. I was literally breathing it all in: clapboard streets, fleets of lobster boats, picturesque towns (we hope they don't get too "quaint"), ocean seaside inns, beaches, harbors, rocks and boulders, eighteenth century Victorian houses, small wooden houses standing precariously above coves, winding roads, and switchback lanes. It was as though we had stepped back into the nineteenth century. A place to remember and be lonesome for.

We ate salads for lunch at a plain restaurant beside the road not far from the ocean. I liked the ordinariness of it, nothing quaint or "cutesy" about it. I felt a sense of authenticity about Cape Ann. It may be foolish to hope it continues to resist the put-on-airs places as attractive as this have, but I hope it stays this way for at least one more visit from me.

We had driven through a countryside and ocean shore of so many stones and boulders that when we approached Gonzagas, the native stone of the Eastern Point Retreat

House seemed a natural part of it all. Not a mansion, more like a manor house—solid, permanent, whole, settled. A welcoming entrance, not too imposing, opened to a small hall and then a very large space—much dark wood and high ceilings. Dignified, magnificent but not intimidating. I loved it and couldn't wait to see our cells.

Joanne and I had rooms next door to each other. They were small—monastic with single beds, a big comfortable lounge chair, a washbowl. The outside wall was all windows under which a shelf that served as a desk ran all the way across the room. Through the window, a grand expanse of green trees and grass. No view of the ocean. No water, but I knew that if I stepped outdoors and turned my body slightly to the left, I could see up the sides of the mountain-like boulder about twenty-five feet off shore, the surf, splashing, shooting sprays of water up the sides.

Those boulders! As the days went on, I focused on them. Blankets in the coves and crevices of that rock mountain. People climbed up into the crooks and crannies onto the flat rocks, lay there in the sun reading or simply looking out at the ocean. During all my days at Gonzagas, I envied the strength and ability of all those young people to climb rocks I couldn't climb. I wanted to do that, too. I wanted to be eighteen or even thirty. It would be life threatening, foolish, even crazy for this old woman to try that. Instead I sat in an Adirondack chair in the shade of a few pine trees, read, wrote and looked out over the ocean. Never mind the pain of envy, I was content, satisfied and happy to be there. With or without Joanne, I strolled—ambled—through densely wooded trails and paths. Wondering what I would find around the next bend, I sat on a rock, not one in the water, trying to hear my inner self. At the same time trying to let go . . .

Silence, even during meals, works magic. It helps the letting go of things that "cloud" the mind. At the same time there is an increased awareness.

When I was younger, I used to divide friends into two groups: one group liked martinis; the other group did not

like martinis. I told Joanne I now have a different measuring
rod: one group of my friends, when I told them I was going
to a silent retreat said, "My god, how dreadful." Another
group said, "How wonderful!"

All meals were served in a large open cafeteria where
one whole glass wall gave us a view of the ocean, a restful
calming scene as small lobster boats moved quietly about. All
meals were vegetarian, fruit and milk available during the day.

*   *   *

Except for one hour with my spiritual advisor each morning,
I was free to read, walk, write, pursue my own path.
Although I am not Catholic, I felt I was absorbing something
spiritual—that I was in a sacred environment. The large room
on the first floor, almost a hall, served as a chapel, a walk-
through to all parts of the building, and as a library. Mass was
offered every afternoon at five o'clock. I never missed a service. Women as well as male priests offered the Mass.

In all the blessed silence and liturgy of the days there
was a strong sense of community. We were, after all, all wor-
shipping the same God. As I sat in a corner reading a book,
the people who passed by smiled at me, as I smiled at everyone I met on a walk or in any room. When Joanne and I talk
about our time at Gonzagas, we always talk about how we
rushed from the Mass to her room where we each had a one-
ounce drink of Scotch before rushing to the cafeteria for our
dinner—rushing to be sure we wouldn't miss a good dessert;
we felt like children.

The hours and days moved swiftly. Two days Nancy
loaned us her car. Joanne took me to visit galleries and restaurants, and one day to the restored home of an early settler.

My hours each morning with the spiritual advisor was
a special time and the real reason why, when I think of being
a writer, I think of Gonzagas. It was during these hours I
spent with Dorothy, a Catholic nun but also a Jungian trained
therapist, that I realized it was all right for me to think of

myself as a writer, that I truly wanted to use some of these extra years given me with "pen in hand." Dorothy asked me many questions, helped me to reach deep within myself, to give authority and credibility to the divine spark each human is given by whatever Gods there be. It was with Dorothy that I recognized how important writing is to me. It's my connection not only to the Edith within, the House of Edith, but to all mankind. I told her that since writing is such a solitary activity and forces me to say no to many things others might expect of me, I had doubts as to the rightness of my choice. Most of my writing is not a matter of an impressive imagination resulting in stories; it's memories and thoughts, writing about my own experiences. I tell myself there is little volunteer work I could do with a kind and loving heart. Maybe I tell myself "I've done my share." Writing feels like my work. It's a part of the integrating "getting it all together" that makes for me a satisfying life. I am never so satisfied, fulfilled, and happy as when I have found the words that convey even a small suggestion of what I feel. Understanding my *feelings*, what they mean, how I feel and act as I do and why, seems to me to be what life is all about. Being human. All of us—children and adults, men and women—cry and laugh, grieve, regret, err, forgive (most important of all). To feel my connection and oneness with other human beings leads to compassion. There is more that connects us than what separates us. All that talk about love is not nonsense. If, since I was a small child, I have felt writing to be the greatest achievement of all, should I not respect that? Should I not see this as credible and okay? Dorothy helped me to see my doubt as a trap.

Although Eastern Point Retreat House is a Catholic institution, Dorothy in no way pushed Catholicism nor pressured me in any way to embrace her personal convictions of the Christ Jesus she believes in. I dutifully read the Scriptural passages from the Holy Bible, and when I admitted that I really could not feel a Jesus walking beside me, she was lovingly understanding and accepted my calling myself a religious Existentialist. She did tell me that I am not really a

Christian, that I am only a Unitarian. Although I can't make the Kierkegardian leap of faith such as Abraham made, I make the same "bet" that Pascal makes and try to live my life as if there is a God, the Creator in control of at least some things. I often think of it as the Loving Universe.

> Hope is the thing with feathers—
> That perches in the soul—
> And sings the tune without the words
> And never stops at all.

That's the way Emily Dickinson sees it.

When the ten days ended and I said good-bye to Dorothy, she kissed me, blessed me, said she'd pray for me and the good life I would lead as a writer, and hoped I would free myself of doubt as to my real work.

Thank you, Dorothy.

Chapter Two

House of Edith

July—At my lady's desk. 4:00 a.m. 77°, humidity 99%

Here I am. One month into my eighty-fifth year. Time to take the idea seriously, the seed planted by the boy on the bench, sprouted in the silence of my head. WHAT IS IT LIKE TO BE MY AGE? My breathing grows short. The distance from the door of my #209 condo to the elevator seems longer than it used to be. No way to know how long I'll be breathing. I can hope it will be long enough to get on paper some idea of what being this age is, long enough to close the cover of the pink notebook I call "Work in Progress." What is it to be me today? For starters, I can say I feel good.

So here I am, sitting at my "lady's desk" in my large bedroom at Kenwood Isles. I love this desk placed in a bay window through which I watch people walking to and from Lund's market, cars and taxis delivering all kinds of people to and from all kinds of places. Now, at four o'clock in the morning, I see stars, stars of light floating about in the black skies. Actually they are not stars. They are the lights of Northwest Airlines planes once again taking over the skies after a long and tedious and annoying strike.

I'm thinking about milestones, images, ideas. Houses and homes. My long life. Houses and homes. House is better—I am thinking of my body as my house. In my house there are many "mansions." Mansions have many rooms. My

11

body. My house. Where I have lived these many years. I was born in this house, built in the womb of my mother. I will die in this house. It has many rooms all safe and connected, held together by a complex structure of bones, sinew, muscles, joints, empty spaces (lots of air), and lots of water. It awesomely adjusts to water, wind, cold, and heat. Sensitive, aware, and an essence I choose to think of as "soul." Never mind the psychologists and scientists who object to the use of that word in this description of a material body. I try to live my life on the assumption that there is an essence, an essence of Edith Elizabeth Johnson Mucke that will go on. The house of Edith.

And so many material houses, so many images alive in my mind. So many shapes and sizes, all the colors, all the rooms—a cell-like room in Greece, my girlhood bedroom in Triumph, Minnesota, the rooms in my grandmother's house in St. Louis Park, all the hotel rooms in Europe and Asia, a tent in Africa. Images merge. Colors run. Pictures. Edges slide under or over.

All of this floating in a very large pool of memories. Is my mind, the pool of memories, like the rest of my body, more water than anything else? Gentle waves and great rushes. High tide. What does all this stuff in the pool mean? How do I, an eighty-five-year-old widow, put all this together? Long journeys. Short paths.

Floating at the very top of the pool of memories, the Bruce Avenue house. Our house. The only house we ever owned. And Paul's image floating over all. Paul's face. He is part of the house.

Paul and I bought the house four years after our marriage in 1940. I lived there fifty-one years, the last five without Paul. Five years during which I came to know the word widow, WIDOW, as one of the most distasteful in the language. I liked the word "wife"—wife gave me a *place*—even when it was used in "just a housewife." After the girls had left home and Paul was gone, I felt I had no real place. I was an outsider. As the years went on and after I moved to Kenwood

Isles, I would come to appreciate the freedom of living alone. But that was later.

High on our list of priorities when Paul and I were looking for a house to buy was location. I refused to look at anything that was not north of Fiftieth Street, east of Highway 100, south of Forty-fourth Street. That meant the Country Club area of Edina, the community where our friends the Millers lived. (We were married in their house. Don was best man at our wedding, and we were married on Dottie's birthday.) I looked at many houses. At that time the market did not offer a great selection in my desired location. There was a white colonial on Moorland that I felt would be just what I wanted—until I saw the inside. What a shock it was. It hadn't been cared for, which I saw as a house that had not been loved and enjoyed. There was a four-bedroom house on Drexel I liked a lot, but the taxes put it out of our reach. When the pleasant (aren't they all?) real estate lady showed me the Bruce Avenue house I immediately fell in love with it. Within a week we were signing papers.

Forty-six years later, on a bright February morning in 1990, Paul, at the age of eighty-seven, drove our Ford Tempo to the First Edina Bank, parked the car in the bank lot, and walked across the street to the Edina Post Office. He mailed a package to our daughter Jane and while reaching for his wallet to pay the postage, fell flat on the floor and died. Just like that. He was dead. Stone dead. I was in California. I was using the last coupon in a book of cheap airplane tickets to make my annual visit to my sister and her husband.

Cathy, our older daughter, was called, and almost had an accident driving to the hospital. (Call 911 and they apparently have no choice but to take you, dead or alive, to a hospital.) It was Cathy who had the heavy burden of phoning me and her sister, Jane. She told me later a voice in her head whispered, "Couldn't we just please wait until tomorrow to do this?" It took me a long time to get over the guilt I felt about not being there. I'd left my husband on Valentine's Day. I was never again to buy a coupon book of plane tick-

13

ets. Cathy tried hard to help me with that later. She continued to remind me that when the taxi picked me up to go to the airport, I'd put my arms around Paul, kissed him goodbye, something I did not do each time he went to the post office or the bank.

Cathy and her husband, Gordy, were at the plane to meet me when I arrived from California. How glad I was to see them! The first-class ticket my brother-in-law, Tryg, had bought for me meant special care on my flight home. An attentive airline representative sat with me, provided free Scotch, a blanket to stop my shivering. I was numb; neither the attention nor the Scotch seemed to do much for me. I hung on to the words, "God is my refuge and strength, a very present help in time of trouble." I repeated the words over and over and over. Cathy, Gordy, and I went directly to the hospital where the body was waiting for us. I had made Cathy promise she would not let them move the body until I got there, although it was supposed to be taken to the Cremation Society. There was some brouhaha about the nurses having harvested Paul's eyes before I got there. Somebody feared I would be "furious." I don't think I even knew it until later. I was in no state to *be* anything.

It is often said that it is sad to realize it takes a death or tragic event to have "everyone together again." But how good it is to have your family "all together" at such hard times. By midnight Jane had arrived from Albuquerque, Jill (Jane's daughter) from New York, Marc and Scott (Cathy's sons) from Reno and Rochester. Leslie, Jane's other daughter, in Paris was out of the question. My sister, Ruth, and her husband, Tryg, in San Diego were with us in spirit every minute. They had performed miracles to get me out of San Diego and on my way home so quickly after the message we received while at the breakfast table.

Sharing our tears, talking about Paul, all remembering together, helped us all to live through that night. I reminded everyone how Paul had died six weeks short of our fiftieth wedding anniversary, and in all that time I could recall his being sick in bed only once—and that, with chicken pox he caught from the girls. Together, we all made some plans for the memorial service we would have at Lakewood Chapel. As for the pain of the mourning, it didn't set in with full force during these moments.

Two years earlier, Paul and I had joined the Cremation Society. We used to talk about death—other people's deaths, never our own—over our dinner coffee, or, more often, at the breakfast room table while reading the morning newspaper. After he retired, it was natural that Paul was interested in reading the obituary columns; names of friends or old colleagues were often to be found there. Natural, too, when I retired at sixty-nine, and he being eleven years older, we attended funerals and memorial services together. This led to conversations about our own funerals. We knew we'd be cremated. Beyond that I only knew for certain that Paul did not like Masonic funerals, hated open coffins and too lengthy "carrying on" as he would say. What he thought about any hereafter, I never heard from him.

It's hard, now that I am eighty-five, not to have Paul across the table, or in the room to ask him if Polly Phillips did die, or am I getting that death mixed up with some other neighbor's death? It is hard this morning, this very morning of the day I write this, not to be able to share with him the news that Margaret Ludwig died last week at ninety-five. She died in Maranatha Home. He would say, were he here, that he'd never heard of that place, and I would say neither had I. I'd go on to say that her husband, Morris, preceded her and the names of the surviving daughters seem familiar—two girls who swam with our girls in all those endless swim meets that Paul, Margaret, and I worked on.

I have this image: Margaret, Paul, and I sit around our family room table with papers spread all over, sharpened pencils in great quantity, ready to perform their function filling in squares and writing the names for the various heats and times of all the kids in the swim meets. Good times we had, Paul as the president of the Amateur Athletic Association. He was the director who set up, registered, announced and administered hundred of meets over seven or eight years. The Ludwig girls, the Knutson kids, Salisbury kids. Wet towels, sweating kids, shivering kids, tired bodies, whistles and guns to start the events. Hot afternoons and long days. Trophies, some with little brass swimmers atop, others with inset brass plates. Butterfly, breast, backstroke, medleys, relays, yelling and screaming and noise. Time sheets stacked on shelves in the basement I cleaned out when I moved from the Bruce Avenue house. Makes me think of the "lumber room" in Kafka.

Cremation Society. And then the ashes. During the year before Paul died, the two of us drove to Lakewood Cemetery to make plans for the disposition of the ashes we would be leaving. We'd discarded, after much consideration, the idea of sprinkling these fragile remains in various places. (Too difficult to choose the right place.) The Lakewood salesman ("salesman" doesn't seem the right word, but if there's another I don't know it) drove us to an area he called Serenity Garden. Lakewood covers a large area; Hubert Humphrey is buried there, so are my parents, many friends and some relatives. Within the confines of the iron fence that surrounds the area is a small quiet pond named by the native Indians, Spirit Lake. Serenity Gardens is on the shore of this lake. Aged oaks and pines, colorful flower beds. The day was cold, skies dark, an icy drizzle. We surveyed the neatly geometric rectangles of real estate ready for granite or marble grave markers and urns. There we stood, my London Fog dripping, Paul's long black overcoat enveloping him. He seemed small.

"I am sad," I said, "to know that we'll both be dead when we are here together."

"Our ashes," he said. And took my hand.

*   *   *

Cremation and ashes settled for us, Cathy, Jane, and I had the funeral arrangements to consider. Neither Paul nor I had any church affiliation. I knew of Paul's dislike of the Masonic rit-

16

ual. Although he'd spent much time with the Masons and loved his work with the Zurah Drum Corps, no Masonic funeral for him!

During my years on campus as director of Continuing Education for Women at the University of Minnesota, I had reported to Harold (Hal) Miller, dean of Continuing Education and Extension. He had a degree in Theology, had at one time hoped to be a minister, and sometimes played a ministerial role. During his graduate school years at Minnesota, Hal earned part of his income parking cars at Gamble Skogmo's, where Paul worked.

Gambles (as it was often called) was a chain store operation selling auto supplies, hardware, and appliances through 300 stores owned in the United States. The organization, like Paul, was born in Fergus Falls, Minnesota, and Paul went to work for Gambles as a young accountant after his first year at Macalaster College. When the company moved its home office from Fergus Falls to Minneapolis, Paul moved too and earned his law degree at the William Mitchell College of Law in St. Paul. He worked for the company as accountant, attorney, comptroller, director, and secretary/ treasurer until he retired forty-five years later.

Back to Hal Miller, who had parked Paul's car mornings and delivered it to him at the end of the work day. He was a friend to both Paul and me. I reached out to him and he agreed to conduct the service for Paul's funeral.

*   *   *

On the morning of the funeral, 19 February 1990, we woke to a white world. The piles of snow in the back yard were ten feet high. The sun was bright. I was glad to know the sun would be pouring through the stained glass windows of the historic, incredibly beautiful, Byzantine chapel at Lakewood. I have no idea what I wore, or even remember thinking about it. I was pleased to know that Ruthie's children, Roxy, Mary, and Beth, were taking care of the food to be served at our house following the service. I went to the basement and brought up the large coffee maker, stood on the stool and brought to the counters bowls and platters, checked on the silverware, and lastly, placed my old King James version of the Bible on a chest on the north wall of the living room. I love that old Bible that my mother and father gave me in 1931, a very long time ago. The leather is as thin and soft as a well-worn glove. The pages seem thinner than onion skin. I opened the pages to the Twenty-third Psalm.

Bouquets of flowers stood on almost every available surface. I remember thinking no wonder we often say, "It smells like a funeral!"

*   *   *

Before the actual service in the chapel, Jane and Jim, Cathy and Gordy, grandchildren Jill, Scott, and Marc, and I were driven to the small rectangle of earth Paul and I had chosen earlier. We stood around in a circle. It was icy cold. All the feet were dressed in Sunday shoes, feet so unfamiliar without their usual canvas sports shoes. In harmony with the frigid temperature, my head and heart must have frozen. I felt numb. I remember looking at Jill with her blond hair, her very short black skirt and the long slim black stockinged legs supported by black pumps with *heels*. How frozen she must be! One of the men in black (from Lakewood I supposed) unscrewed a cover from a metal urn, said something about ashes or was it remains? Remains . . . such a strange word for that small portion of matter that was once a part of my husband. The Cremation Society man said a prayer and maybe we all said the Lord's Prayer. The metal container now enclosing the ashes was placed in the marble marker waiting for Paul's name and the dates of his life on this earth. I yielded to the impulse to kneel and kiss the cold marker. Marc still talks about how worried he was that his grandmother's lips would be frozen to the stone.

*   *   *

Then back to the chapel. The news of Paul's death and notice of the funeral had appeared in the *Star Tribune*. Many people came. Paul was a truly independent soul, unconventional. When he was still serving as a corporate officer for Gamble Skogmo's, he gave up wearing neckties and became known to friends and strangers as "the man who never wears a tie." Now, at the funeral, many people came without their ties, saying, "I'm *not* wearing a tie, in honor of Paul." We all smiled and appreciated the gesture.

We, small group that we were, the mourning family, were seated in the front of the chapel, off to the side, protected from the eyes of the congregation.

"Hal Miller's words were just right." That's what one of my friends said to me after the service. And they were. I remember little of the service, but I made it through. Afterwards, we, the family, in the entry of the church, greeted and thanked visitors for coming, breathed in the cold outside air. Shivering and talking about the cold, we drove home.

At our house, the dining room table was laid out with sandwiches, meats, cheese, potato salad, cakes, and cookies. People were sitting and standing. It was comforting, and I was happy to see so many friends. I was grateful for everyone who came. Since that occasion, I have attended many more funerals and receptions—many that I would have skipped had I not experienced that day. The girls and I all say that we never realized how much it means to mourners to have a friend attend a funeral. Participation in the service is a great gift.

Then the guests were gone. The table still heavy with food, ham for sandwiches for days to follow. Stories in which Paul was the central figure continued to fill the occasional silent spaces. Smiles and sighs. All this tradition, the presence of beloved human beings. The details had been handled. The work of our hands numbly performing, reacting. We'd been given the strength, and it was over. Paul. He was gone. This then was the beginning of a long black tunnel, the mourning.

Chapter Three

Mourning

August, 11:00 P.M.—Kenwood Isles, my study desk

I woke this morning to a dull gray sky. Damp and still. Not a leaf stirring in any one of the elm or linden trees that line Humboldt Avenue. August is not my favorite month. I tell myself on mornings like this that my favorite month, September, comes next. There's something wonderful about September. Like everything wakes up—the start of the school year, new beginnings. Today I had lunch with a friend I like and enjoy. But she has just lost a husband, and there's something not easy about that for me. I remember my own losses and how I often felt that there are some days when anything anybody says is all wrong. I would like to help her but there's little I can do. My memories come forth. Long black tunnels of grief. That I have negotiated this journey twice (the deaths of my mother and my husband) does not help me to find words. But I met her for lunch, told her I am thinking about her. I told her that it will not last forever. She thanked me.

*   *   *

Once upon a time, a long time ago, shortly after my mother died, I thought I'd used up a lifetime of tears, dried up the very source of tears, and maybe I'd never need to cry again. (I was to learn after Paul's death many years later that the supply is infinite). Mother died in April. She was sixty-four. I was

21

thirty-seven. The first of May, Paul and I took our children to the west coast of Florida for our annual spring vacation. I thought I was pretty settled down and had cried enough and was happy to be on the beach. (I smile now to realize how naive I was—mourning is no short-term challenge.) I walked into a drug store on Madeira Beach for a tube of toothpaste. As I walked down the aisle toward the pharmacy section, a rack of cards for Mother's Day caught my eye. I stopped, read the sentimental but seemingly heartfelt messages. They all seemed sincere and true to me. Tears rolled down my cheeks. I could not stop the flow. I again knew the homesickness for my mother. I knew the torturing terrorizing pain of my loss. I had not known anything about how long this could go on! I knew again the finality of death. I would never see her again. I walked back to my family outside in the white Florida sunshine, trying hard to be and feel *normal*. Surprise *attacks* I called them. Unexpected they always were. And they came to me in the same way after I thought I'd accepted the fact of Paul's death.

During the summer after Paul's death in 1990: In the Gellert Hotel on the River Danube in Budapest, Hungary, Jane and I were in a posh upper hotel room with French windows open to the summer night air. We'd had a lovely day sightseeing in friend Johanna's old city, a haute cuisine dinner, violins playing . . . All of a sudden sitting on our bed, I began shaking with sobs. I tried to explain to Jane why I was crying. I tried to tell her how hard it was for me to overcome the feeling of guilt I suffered, the sorrow and sadness I felt about being in California when Paul died, how Cathy had had to take on the burden of telephoning her and me, and how sad I was not to have been with him at the end of his life. Again and again, she reminded me of how Cathy had comforted me by reminding me that when I left for California, I'd kissed him good-bye and how I didn't kiss him good-bye every time he went to the post office and how I would not have gone to the post office and bank with him that morning, how Cathy found comfort in knowing that she'd been able to touch her father's body while it was still warm. I carried on somewhat hysterically about how sorry and guilty I felt because I had been distressed and angry many times during our shared lives because he had not acted exactly as I would have wished him to act. I wanted him to forgive me for every single time I'd not been appreciative of his kindness and his thoughtfulness and the times I'd been angry because I felt he wasn't putting me FIRST, when I'd been disturbed about his being less than perfect in my eyes . . . I was indulging in an angry lamentation of my own shortcomings. I knew while I was putting myself through all this pain that I was making the evening hard for Jane, but I couldn't seem to calm down, couldn't stop the tears. As I write all this (years later; it is now nine years since his death), I can almost smile. It's a wry smile and somewhat shamefully my lips turn upward. An *almost* smile, knowing guilt and pardon, love and forgiveness, forgiveness of self and others is all a part of the mourning. Remembering and forgetting. Knowing and not knowing. Mourning seems to cover the whole emotional scale. It's not up and down, in and out, it's a wheel going round and round. Finally, I recognized it's a spiral going forth, trying and, finally, breaking through the tunnel. Tears. Maybe they are a lubricant helping us to go forward to that small pinpoint of light at the end of the tunnel. Bless the tears.

*   *   *

I am remembering a day some weeks after Paul's death, when Cathy, my beloved firstborn daughter, walked in the back door of our house, into the family room of our Bruce Avenue house, in she came, tears streaming down her cheeks, her eyes red, rage disfiguring her beautiful face.

"Can't anyone understand, Mother? They don't understand. If one more person comes up to me and tells me she knows how I feel, I may just haul off and hit her. Don't they understand? I'LL NEVER SEE MY DADDY AGAIN! I'LL NEVER TALK TO DADDY AGAIN AND HE'LL NEVER TALK TO ME!" There was nothing I could say. I was having as hard a time with this despair as she was.

When Cathy came in with that explosion of rage, another memory flashed before me.

My mother died in 1951. As I walked up the stairs of Abbott Hospital on a cold winter morning, I was surprised to realize how glad I was that she was still alive. She was dying. She knew it. I knew it. She was in great pain. It was hard to see her suffering. (Is cancer the worst of deaths?) But I was glad to know she was alive, clear in her head, despite the morphine, and I would see and talk with her. (She died three months later in her own house, in her own bed. Papa, her sister Anna, and I were with her.) I see myself two hours later. I am standing on the corner of Nicollet Avenue and Seventh Street. People are entering and leaving Donaldson's Department Store. I cannot understand how people are crossing the street, walking in and out of the revolving doors, buying perfume, buying stockings, letting everything go on as usual. I remember the tears, the dry sobs, the disorientation, the impossible finality of my never being able to talk with her again. I remember only the pain, even terror. I survived, twice. I remember thinking I never would. I survived, and my daughters survived.

*   *   *

Now, here I sit. Nine years and six months since Paul died. I survived the two dark tunnels. Our daughters survived. That's how I know the pain does not last forever.

How do we survive? The cards, the flowers, the letters, and the loving touch of friends help and comfort. It is, however, a journey one has to make alone. Being together sometimes helps. Sharing the pain. Jane stayed with me a few weeks after Paul's funeral. Cathy came for dinner once a week for a while. We went through drawers and some of Paul's things together. There were some tears, some laughter, some smiles—a small box Cathy as a Brownie Scout had painted, containing tiny baby teeth father fairy had treasured, ballet costumes in a closet, the guns we knew Paul would want

Scott to have, dusty volumes of law books from college, hunting clothes, a white satin sash Paul had worn in Shrine Drum Corps parades. Letters from me, cards from the girls.

Was the first year the hardest? Or was the second the hardest? I don't know. Does it matter?

I attended a few sessions of a grief support group at Fairview Hospital. I didn't stay long, feeling after four sessions I was in better shape than many of the persons there. One woman told us that her husband had been dead for three years and she had not as yet been able to shed a tear. I could *hear* the quiet sympathy being felt by members in the circle. God's gift, tears.

*   *   *

When Paul fell in the post office, he was wearing a dark green wool beret I'd brought him from Scotland. When it was returned to me by the hospital, I held it, touched the stiff blood-stained wool. I held it and knew I could never part with it. The Edina Cleaners did their best to remove the almost black stains. The beret rests at the bottom of my dresser drawer. It will be there when someone cleans out my condo.

Smell may be the hardest of all our senses to describe. What is more intimate than the smell of someone's body? (This is no place for *fragrance* or *odor*!) I could not bear to give up the sheets in our bed that continued to suggest Paul's living presence. I slept with those sheets for a very long time. Who would care if they wore out before I gave them up? Whose business was it but mine? When I did wash them, I found myself going into his closet where hung two flannel shirts he'd worn that had not been laundered. The feel of them, the smell of them, brought his presence—a kind of comfort.

There are memories time never dulls.

When I retired in 1983, I'd lived sixty-nine years. Paul was eighty, fifteen years retired. Fifteen years. He died seven years later. We had seven years of retirement together. For fifteen years while I worked on campus, he kept house. I never felt any guilt about leaving him those years because I knew he loved having the house to himself. "Who doesn't?" he once remarked. Dolores, a good woman from Le Seur, who'd been our helper for years (we called her "the Cleaning Lady") continued to give our house a good cleaning every two weeks. Paul took over the daily housekeeping. Actually, he was always a better housekeeper than I was. Within a few months, he was cooking dinner every evening.

With smiles, I remember one evening at dinner: his face took on an expression familiar to me—the look his face wore when he was about to say something that wasn't easy for him to say. Spouses, children, parents learn to recognize that particular look.

"Edith," he began, "I wish that when you wash out the little pan you boil your egg in, you'd see that it's dry before you put it away."

Paul had the characteristics I often assign to accountants and bookkeepers: paper money in his billfold always had all the heads on top, pencils in his desk drawer had all the points facing the same direction. He was much neater than I.

In my journal there is an entry dated 19 February 1986 that reads:

> Edith: I had an idea. I'm going to put all the big brown grocery bags in the slots for trays.
>
> Paul: (no comment)
>
> (Several days later)
>
> P: Now, about the grocery bags. I want you to use the bags from Lunds for the garbage and the ones from Country Club for trash, waste basket trash.
>
> E: Okay. (goes to get the bags)
>
> P: And you will notice that I have arranged them so that the Lunds bags are on the left and the others on the right.
>
> E: (mentally, on her way upstairs.

Okay, Lunds bag for the trash—no, Lunds for garbage. Goes to get the bags.) Wouldn't it be better if the folds were on the outside? How about Jerry's Grocery bags?

P: Obviously they are for garbage. Wouldn't it be better if you had just left them where they were? All under the sink?

E: (to herself. Dear Paul, bless his sense of order.)

Dear God, bless his sense of order . . . Often he would surprise me. One evening, while we were having our usual drink before dinner, he with his bourbon, me with my scotch, he said, "I changed the sheets on our beds this morning. I thought you would like not to have to remember that tomorrow is Saturday; and you will not have to change the sheets." It seems that often I forgot to do this Saturday morning and would end up doing it Sunday night.

While Paul kept house, he was also active in civil and community affairs. He served on committees appointed by the mayor of Edina; he belonged to the Edina Historical Society (serving as secretary/treasurer was a natural for him); he was active in the organization of the AARP chapter in Edina; and he joined a needlepoint class, the only man in the class. After his death, the teacher of the class wrote me a much-treasured letter telling me how much she and other women in the class enjoyed his being with them. He used to say, "If Rosie Greer can needlepoint, so can I." I used to love coming home from campus seeing him, sunlight streaming into the family room, working on his handiwork. (What a wonderful word is *handiwork*. I felt sad when his eyes, and probably his fingers, made it necessary for him to give up his needle pointing.)

Paul and I never lost our interest in our bodies or each other's bodies. It was our sex life, his presence in my bed, that I so sorely missed after he died. Paul never lost his interest nor his potency in making love. Yes, yes, I say to the counselors

27

and people who study sex and aging. There is sex after seventy and after eighty. Paul died at eighty-seven, and we had made love the week before. And no Viagra.

It was during those seven years that I began seriously to write. Friends who were published writers encouraged me not to give up. George Hage at one point said never give up until you have had at least thirty rejections. Paul felt bad every time a rejection letter arrived in the mail. He felt even worse than I did because he hadn't heard as much about the difficulty of publishing as I had. I wrote an essay on "Ironing" that appeared in *Hurricane Alice* and an early version of "The Store" that appeared in a Grand Forks, North Dakota, journal, *The Plainswoman*. Encouraging as those publications were, I continued to merit nothing but rejections on major projects until after Paul's death. I am sorry about that. He would have been so happy with me.

Paul's hands. I see him standing at a long counter in our large kitchen. He has come from Lund's Market and is emptying a brown grocery sack of food. He places each item on the counter—the to-be-refrigerated items on a far side of the counter, cans and bottles together, packages in a separate section. Wide fingers, blunt nails at the ends of wide fingers, palms flat, he folds the sack in its original folds, pleats, and slides them into their proper vertical slot below the cupboard. Later, when it's time for a new trash bag under our sink, he will slowly, deliberately fold the top edges outward and carefully line the basket. Tears came to my eyes the day I stood in the kitchen when he was no longer there and the scene flashed before my eyes. His hands.

We had in our family room a couch and a love seat. How often during that first year after his death, I'd be reading on my love seat, and I would sense him on the couch. I'd look over and be surprised for a moment, a very short moment, not to see Paul over there, body stretched long, not to see his newspaper or book or hear the television.

Three times that first year I experienced Paul's presence. I thought I heard his footsteps coming up the stairs and felt or saw him standing beside my bed. It was real enough to cause me to turn on the light to prove he was not actually there. Twice I saw him sitting near me on my bed. Both times my response was the same—turning on the light. Hallucination? Imagination? Who knows?

As I dreamed of my mother after her death, so I often dreamed of Paul, and still do—less often as time goes on. We are together or he is part of what I am experiencing in the dream. Then I wake up and am forced to go through the acceptance of the terrible knowledge that he is dead, as my mother is dead, as my father is dead. Gone. I'll never see them again. I'll never see Paul again.

Mourning is no short journey. Pain is a constant companion. Little by little, moment by moment, the pain eases and now after all this time, I can say it does not last forever.

Chapter Four

Matin

September, 6:15 A.M.—47 degrees, 91% humidity

At the desk in my bedroom. Body still and warm, having just crawled out from under the white comforter that once covered Paul and me. A new day. This day. A gift. One more beautiful day. Gift of life. Twenty-four hours of it all mine. Nothing on my calendar. No place I have to be at a special hour. No one invited to enter my space this day. A day all mine. Nothing hurts. Feel wonderful. At two o'clock this morning, I woke to use the bathroom. Very much awake. I warmed a cup of milk and dumped a splash of scotch in the cup—careful to make it less than an ounce, for flavor, I thought, and an invitation to more sleep. Four hours later I lay looking at the ceiling, thinking about Louise Bogan's *Journey Around My Room*. I'd like to write a piece about a mental journey around this bedroom. Not today. So many things I always want to do the very first thing in the morning. The long list includes:

(1) Turn on my Jon Kabat Zinn meditation tape. That means staying under the warm cocoon another half hour and sometimes more sleep.

(2) Or I might splash my face, throw on shorts and a shirt and walk the two blocks to Lake of the Isles where I would stretch my arms high and wide, say good morning to the lake, the Canada geese, the skies and trees, and the water, walk to a bridge or a certain bench or maybe half the way

around the lake, wondering when to turn back or go ahead.

(3) Or in the same clothes I could walk to the YWCA just next door, take a place on one of the large bright blue mats and go into the stretching routine my trainer, Michael, has taught me, after which I'd do the weight-lifting routine with the purple 4.5 pound weights.

(4) Or I might read. The pile is high: Jon Kabat Zinn's *Wherever You Go There You Are*, followed by a period of meditation. I consider this inner directed period of meditation an antidote to my tendency to hurry all the time. Hurry and rushing are enemies that cause me to lose things, make mistakes, cause confusion. The stillness of meditation feels like an appreciation of time I have been given, a move toward patience.

More books: Don Pasos' *Manhattan* is a 1925 book we are reading in Johanna Kheim's literature course; *Everything But . . .* , a newly published autobiography by my longtime friend Joy Davis; or *Over the Hill*, written by a sixty-year-old teacher who went to Hungary as a Peace Corps worker when she retired; or Louise Glueck's beautiful poetry in *Meadowlands*, the work for my Noname Reading book group.

*　　　　*　　　　*

Or I could do what I am doing now: face a large legal-sized pad of lined yellow paper. Yellow which, writer Trish Hampl points out, is a warm and friendly color, bringing to the writer an experience less scary or terrifying than the first piece of square-cornered smooth white paper atop the stack of paper on the desk.

Sometimes when words are like a waterfall in my brain and I must get them on paper immediately before I lose them, when I am thinking of a special person or have an idea that seems to me insightful (most often it isn't anything new), I rush fast because my fingers are energy loaded. Sometimes I rush because I think I have a poem singing in my soul. (Whatever that means—usually I have the "tune but not the words"—thanks Emily D.)

This morning I took time for consideration and then

knew an explosion of praise and gratitude for the gift of life I am given. September, my favorite month—the trees, the color of the trees, the gold of memories of other Septembers. Maybe this really is the "Best Season of my Life." My mind is not "clouded by unnecessary things." The sky is pink, but not for long. The sky is a gift I have given myself by buying this condo. An elegant display of gold trees; sky floods every room. I look with wonder at the linden trees. Only one would be enough. One, and I have five! I don't need the whole North Shore or New England. One is a miracle, and I have all five. I am truly at one with the world.

And then I remember the phone call two days ago from my cousin Jim Richardson in California. He gave me the news that his older brother Bill is "no longer with us." Bill took his life by shooting himself in the head, in the back yard of his San Diego home. His wife, Eleanor, was on her way to the airport to pick up her relatives, coming to a reunion. "Forever considerate," said Jim. "Eleanor would have family with her when she found the body."

My Aunt Anna, Bill's mother, was always close to her sister Bessie, my mother. The sisters always talked of how Bill and Edith were both so like their father, Bill's and my grandfather, that Bill and Edith always had their noses in books. Both "addicted" to pen and paper.

So many summers ago . . . when Mother took Ruth and me to Stillwater to visit our Richardson relatives . . . We hunted for frogs in the wetlands, we swam together in the St. Croix River. Ruth and I, having no brothers, loved playing ball with the Richardson boys, the closest thing to brothers we had. In the last few years, Bill suffered from macular degeneration so far advanced he was practically blind; a prostate cancer had invaded his bones. I didn't have any trouble with his decision to end it all. But now I will never talk to Bill again. I will never write to him, nor will he write to me. We never lived in the same town. He was male, I female, he was ten years younger than I was. But there was always a magical something between us. About fifteen years ago, Bill and I had a long talk when he was driving me from his mother's to a party at a seaside cafe. We laughed and talked quietly, the two of us, shared memories and "wisdom" we felt we'd picked up along our separate journeys.

I will never see Bill again. I will never have any true closure on my relationship with him. They were all such beautiful boys—lushly virile, tall, handsome, brown-skinned bodies, prominent noses, sparkling brown eyes. Bill had an illustrious career in the U.S. Navy. We both earned college degrees much later in our lives than other people; devoured that knowledge. He wrote a book about Portuguese sailors who settled in California, made their living as fisherman, founded fishing communities that grew to become cities.

The finality of death. I will never get used to it. I will always have trouble accepting it.

*   *   *

Out my window, an orange school bus stops at the corner. The day begins. I never close the blinds in this room. Skies with stars or planes at night. Skies now turning blue, and a paler blue. The orange bus. September. Burnt orange leaves and a few red later in the month. September. Fourth grade with Miss Jensen and my learning the multiplication tables because I'd missed them when I skipped third grade. High school and freshman year with brown-and-white saddle shoes and bobby sox, falling in love, walking through crackling dusty leaves, holding the hand of a young lover, the University campus, my own children going off . . . Life goes on. A miracle every day.

And now I will do the Qigong, have my breakfast, go to the lake, and live this day, head in the clouds, feet on the ground. Have a good day, Edith Elizabeth Johnson Mucke. Harm no one. Joy cometh—not only in the morning—let it be all day.

Chapter Five

Kenwood Isles

October, 60 degrees, 50% humidity

October is my second favorite month of the year. As I eat my breakfast of Quaker oatmeal (I love to cook it; it takes one minute) sprinkled with Kellogg's All Bran and swimming in luxurious two-percent milk (I can't bring myself to accept that pure skimmed bluish stuff), I am looking at the Midas glow of the trees viewed from my balcony. I am remembering an earlier October, an October day that was the beginning of my ownership of this home at Kenwood Isles, the real beginning of my life as a Woman Alone, radiantly grateful for the gift of Life.

*   *   *

"I don't know just how long I'll be in this house," I said to Jane. When my book, a memoir of growing up in Triumph, Minnesota, came out in June 1994 and I celebrated my eightieth birthday, Jane did not come home, but here she was now, sitting in our living room on Bruce Avenue. It was mid-October 1994. We'd been talking about adolescence—hers and Cathy's and mine. We were talking too about Paul, her "Daddy," who had now been gone almost five years.

"I don't know how long I'll be in this house," I went on, "but I don't think it makes sense for me to spend the rest of my life here. People keep telling me I'll know when it's right to move on, but how will I know? I've seen people who waited too long."

"Where can you imagine moving?" questioned Jane. "You and Daddy had that place on York Avenue in mind."

"No way would I ever move there! Our name came up on the list, the long waiting list. We said we weren't ready, and it might have been right for the two of us, but not for me alone. It's hard to think of leaving this house or this neighborhood, but there is one place I think I'd like to live—the old West High School building was torn down, and in its place now is a condominium. Uptown area. I lived there—in four different red-brick buildings—when I worked as a secretary before I was married. Ruth and I used to take the street car from Gramma's when we were children and visited in St. Louis Park. I went to business school there. It would be a great location."

"Uptown, where the action is."

We talked about how when my sister, Ruthie's, husband, Tryg, died, the girls had suggested I invite Ruth to come and share my house. I told Jane how Ruth and I laughed at that suggestion. We'd often talked about how we could never live together, how fortunate we would probably never have to . . . We loved taking trips together, loved visiting each other and our almost daily phone conversations. We knew ourselves and each other better than ever to agree to give up our individual independence.

I asked Jane, "Would you be willing to take a part of this precious day" (her visit was getting close to the last days), "and drive with me over to Lake and Hennepin to take a look at Kenwood Isles?" So off we went.

We drove around the south and east shores of Lake Calhoun where the girls had learned to swim, where we'd had noon-day picnics on Thomas Beach. October is often Minnesota's most glorious season. That year it really was. Trees were beginning to shed their lush summer clothing, showing off the many shades of green and fading greens, bronze, yellow, brilliant orange, pinks, and even a suggestion of amethyst and gold. The sun was shining; its rays from the west gave the trees and the lake that particular magic that moves me.

Arriving at the Kenwood Isles condominiums, we walked on a red carpet under a long canopy into a lobby, and approached a gentle gray-haired woman with a smiling face at the reception desk. Was there anything here we could see? A real estate agent standing by overheard our conversation and offered to show us a couple of condos he had for sale. We were impressed by the layout but were not interested in the two one-bedroom condos he showed us; I knew that I wanted a two-bedroom unit. After he left, the woman at the desk, Evelyn, suggested that if we wanted to see a two-bedroom unit, a gentleman had one to rent, and we might like to take a look at that.

"The owner," said Evelyn, "is not interested in selling this unit, but he never locks the door, and if you'd like to go in and look at it, you may do so."

We couldn't move fast enough.

We opened the door to unit 209. We were dazzled by a glorious display of golden foliage, magnificent shade trees across the street wearing October colors, sun shining through the three glass doors. Moving freely and happily through the whole place—living room, kitchen, two bedrooms, two baths, we were awed by the sense of light and space. We sat down on the floor, facing the balcony with its view of tree-shaded Humboldt Avenue—dark red-brick, sturdy, weathered houses speaking to us of long-settled hospitable city homes, tradition, and warmth. The walls and ceiling around us were sparkling white. I saw a celebration of light and space. With great conviction, I said to Jane, "If I could live here, I think I could bear the pain of leaving our house." She shared my enthusiasm. It all seemed perfect.

Before we left the building, pleasant Evelyn, at the desk, gave us names, addresses, and phone number of, not only the owner, Ed Settevig, but his daughter. In the weeks following, we had telephone conversations with Mr. Settevig and with his daughter. Would it be foolish to take a chance on renting? Would it be foolish to risk paying $1,200 a month for a time with only the hope that it might lead to buying the place? The more I thought about it, the more I talked about it, the more "right" it seemed.

On a cloudy, cold November day I paid a visit to Ed Settevig, who was living at the Masonic Home. Unsure of the location, unfamiliar with the Bloomington area, I called a taxi to take me there for my three o'clock appointment. There was such a sense of foreboding in the skies, that when the cab driver got lost, I began to feel this whole venture must be doomed. While the cab driver drove into a gas station to get directions, I began to take comfort at least in the idea that I'd listened to the voices within to call Yellow Cab instead of driving myself.

It was almost four o'clock when I finally walked through the long halls of the Masonic Home to Ed Settevig's room. He'd been waiting for me in the lobby and finally gave up. I have always hated being late, and I was very nervous.

I arrived at his room. There sat Ed. Although he was in a wheelchair, he gave the impression of being a tall man. Long and lean type. A narrow, lined face, hair on his head, and round glasses sliding down a broad nose. A good strong voice, betraying no evidence of displeasure at my tardy appearance. He certainly did not look ninety-two years old. Parkinson's disease was what kept him in a wheelchair.

"When you go to see my father," his daughter Dorothy had suggested, "bring him a copy of your book. He is always interested in small towns and people growing up in them." I followed her suggestion, brought a copy of *Beginning in Triumph*, inscribed for him,

> For Ed, whose wonderful
> vibrations fill the rooms
> of Condo 209 at Kenwood
> Isles. Enjoy!
>
> Edith

I gave him the book and looked about the room—a small bed, a night stand, a desk, shelves filled with books and papers and pictures.

Despite the atmosphere of the day and my state of apprehension, the visit went well. "This is a nice place," I said, "and I'm sure the Masons see that you are well taken care of." He thanked me for the book and seemed very pleased. I was not convinced that he saw well enough to read as much as Dorothy had said, but never mind, he acted very pleased.

Ed showed me photographs of the log cabin in North Dakota where he'd been born, photographs of himself taken with celebrity figures from the State of Minnesota and Masonic dignitaries. My husband had been an active Shriner, so Ed and I found much to talk about. He talked about his wife and how he missed her, how they'd given up a very large house to move to Kenwood Isles. He told me the story of his life, how he'd left North Dakota after establishing a successful business there, but got "mixed up with the wrong kind of people, drink and all of that . . ." He finally hopped a train and came to Minneapolis where he won the battle over drink and started another business which turned out to be very successful. (I think it was a paint business.)

He added that his daughter Dorothy likes both me and my daughter Jane very much. He was obviously in a frame of mind to make a good deal. I relaxed.

"Trust," said Ed, "that's the key. And I trust you, and you trust me. I've done business like this for years, and it works better than paying lawyers hundreds of dollars."

Ed asked me if I could type, and I said, "Of course." I would be glad to type up our agreement. He assured me he had a good machine, and after a bit of fumbling about in a closet, he brought it out. I wish I had a movie of our getting this agreement on paper. The typing of the document (Get this, DOCUMENT with neither a "whereas " nor "first person") was not a simple matter. The machine was not only old but many keys did not work properly. When he moved the table to give me more room, we knocked a tape machine off, and a basket of candy flew all over. Now, while I was trying to make friends with the typewriter, he was struggling with the tape player, which he finally got to work, meaning that he would play for me a tape on which he read poetry when he gave a short talk to a group of people. On the tape he recited by heart Kipling's *Gunga Din* and a few other familiar (but not to me) poems. Nurses kept walking in and walking out. Did they wonder what in the world was going on?

Here is what I typed up and we both signed:

> I, Edith Mucke, agree to pay to Ed Settevig the amount of $1,200 per month beginning the first of June, 1995. Occupancy as of this day if desired. This includes garage and maintenance fee. At the end of one year, I have the option to buy from his daughter, Dorothy Masewicz, the condo at a price to be agreed upon between Dorothy and me. I have the privilege of moving in any time before the first, but rent payments do not begin until June first. Ed agrees to give Edith the patio furniture. Signed this 30th day of November, 1994.

After we had both signed, we had a nurse come in and witness our signatures. I had completed it when he insisted I add the line about the patio furniture. "Good stuff," he said, " and even the patio carpet you can have."

It was really a wonderful afternoon. I liked the guy. Some pretty classy stuff in the scrap books. He felt bad we couldn't go to dinner someplace. He invited me to have dinner there, but I said I had other commitments. I told him I would be glad to have lunch with him and Dorothy some day.

I told him how heroic he was to have given up the drinking all by himself and done so well with his life, to have had the courage to run away from what he knew was a bad scene. One of the poems he had read on the tape was about putting a hand on the shoulder. I put my hand on his shoulder and patted his back. He kept saying he hoped I'd be as happy in the condo as he and his wife had been.

Leaving the house on Bruce Avenue.

He told me how he happened to buy the condo. They lived in a fifteen-room house, and one day he found his wife sitting on the basement steps crying because her legs hurt so much. And that's when he decided they'd give up that house with all the stairs and all the stuff.

41

I put my arms around him and kissed him good-bye. He had tears in his eyes when I left. And so did I. How could anyone doubt that this was all divinely ordained? I went home with the small but important piece of paper that night.

Knowing that I looked forward to living in Uptown in an apartment I liked very much eased the pain I knew I would feel about leaving my house. I was busy thinking about what I would take with me, what I would get rid of—sell, or give to the children. Judy O'Brien who lived two houses north of me was a friend and a real estate agent. I had trust in her judgment and her integrity. She helped me in many ways—moral and emotional support, advice about how to get my house ready to show, what price to ask. She took care of the showing, and the couple who bought the house saw it the second or third day it was on the market. Best of all, they did not want to move in until the first of June. That seemed to confirm my sense that this whole thing was being divinely administered.

I'd sold my house and had a place that would be my new home! I would enjoy the summer in our old house.

My niece Roxy, who is a designer, had seen the condo. I showed it to my sister. I showed it to several friends. Everybody approved. It never entered my mind that I would not one day be able to buy this condo. If there were friends who thought I was out of my mind to spend money replacing the carpet without a definite assurance that I would one day own the place, they were kind enough not to tell me. I gave Roxy a key. She made a sketch of the floor plan and took measurements. I had new carpeting laid. We decided that building a bookcase along a diagonal wall in the living dining area would be a great addition. But, warned her attorney husband Bill, before making that move, I should really get approval from the present owner. And also, he pointed out, the purchase option I'd written into the agreement between myself and Ed didn't have any validity unless there was a dollar amount spelled out. So, Bill suggested, when I make another trip out to see Ed Settevig to get permission to build in bookcases, I'd better see if I could get something in writing about the purchase price if and when the option is recognized. That meant another trip to get something settled with Ed.

Meanwhile, Ed and I felt everything was settled and we had become friends. He invited me to have lunch with him at the Shriner's Club where he wanted me to meet some of his friends. I accepted, and we all met for lunch and conversation. Ed was pleased to have his friends meet the woman who would be living in a place with which they were familiar. Paul's having been an active Shriner made conversation easy. Ed took great pride in showing me displays (under glass) of gifts he'd given to the club.

However, my second visit to talk with Ed at the Masonic Home was not as easy as our initial meeting. While I had assumed that I would start paying rent the first of June, Ed thought I should pay $1,200 a month from the date of signing, and that I should, at the very least, give him a check that day for $2,400. We didn't exactly argue. I think it's fair to say we talked a great deal. Maybe bargaining is the exact word. It is true to say that we both ended up crying—he because his wife was dead and he was alone; I because I was frustrated, confused, disappointed. Meanwhile, a nurse kept coming in and going out. Maybe he gave in by agreeing that I did not have to pay from that very day, but that if I gave him a check for $2,400, we would agree on the option dollars being less than his original investment. I wrote him a check for $2,400. After all that, I accepted his invitation to go downstairs to the coffee shop and have an ice cream sundae. As we walked out the door and down the hall, the nurse must have been relieved to see this pitiful pair whom she'd observed crying in Ed's room walk to the elevator like two normal persons. We ate our ice cream covered with shiny chocolate sauce and parted on a happy note.

When my Yellow Cab came to take me home, I was exhausted, feeling forlorn—not really abandoned but pitiful and alone. The cab driver was not unknown to me. He'd driven me many times. His name was George (I suppose it still is), an Englishman, an actor who, when we were once held up in a traffic mess, quoted me long passages from Shakespeare's *Henry IV*, a very interesting likeable guy. I was in no mood to listen to Shakespeare or anything else. My experience with cab drivers is that many have a sixth sense about when to talk and when not to talk. He maybe sensed my state. He told me about his hard day and from then on, remained quiet.

My homecoming did little to cheer me up. I was alone, wretched, and miserable. The house was cold and empty. Would Cathy and Jane and Bill think me a crazy old woman? I didn't even have $2,400 in my checking account. I would have to move money around the first thing in the morning. I sat down in what used to be Paul's chair, and let the tears flow. How would all this turn out?

Chapter Six

The Best Laid Plans

November—cold, gray, damp

It's a cold, gray day. 14 November. We've had an easy, glorious fall. Leaves of yellow, gold, rust . . . earthy shades. Much sunshine and blue skies. People have been talking to each other about the blessed weather. Not today. The wind is cold and mean. Tired leaves on walks and lawns are not dancing. They are damp, sodden, and depressed.

I'm thinking about black tunnels. How do I define a black tunnel? How does my mental perspective define a black tunnel? Which are the big ones? The small ones? Are some more narrow than others? Do some have spikes around the inside? I'm not a mathematician nor an accounting clerk. I just like to keep track of things.

The background is all set. I'd sold my house. I would move the first of June; agreements with Ed Settevig were all confirmed and we planned to close both deals on the first of June. But . . .

. . . the best laid plans of mice and men . . .

I had worked through the long period of painful mourning. I'd finished the book I'd been seriously working on since my retirement, and even had it published—a dream come true. I played bridge weekly, took a water aerobics class,

traveled to Germany and Austria, visited granddaughter
Leslie in Paris, enjoyed much time with daughter Cathy and
her family. I had learned that my life did not stop with Paul's
death. And I continued to take Johanna's literature classes.

I was grateful for the health, energy, and enthusiasm to
be able to say, "My Life is good." My oncologist had told me
that my 1979 mastectomy (the pathologists in the lab of the
University Hospital had found the smallest cancer cell they'd
ever seen) left me totally clean, and since I'd been carefully
watched ever since, he could tell me, "You will never die of cancer; something else will get you first." I'd found a completely
satisfying home at Plymouth Congregational Church. I'd joined
a spiritual growth class led by Nancy Baltins, a fine leader in that
church. I'd made new friends. I'd worked to get my house in
proper condition for the sale I would have before moving.

*   *   *

And then it happened. A gray Wednesday morning on the
third of February I stood at my bedroom window, wondering, trying to decide, whether I should drive to Johanna's
class downtown or park my car at Forty-fourth and France as
I often did, and take the bus downtown. I can't remember the
why of that uncertainty. Were there icy spots on the road? I
finally decided to drive.

When I drove to Forty-fourth I saw two friends
standing on the corner waiting for the bus. I stopped, invited
them to climb in. They did, both in the back seat. I drove my
usual route, around a part of Lake Calhoun and then east on
Thirty-sixth Street. At Lyndale I made a left turn, saw a huge
white car fly toward me, and then . . . a head on crash. It's
quite impossible for me to understand, but from the facts
given, it is hard for me not to think it was my fault. God bless
the no-fault insurance laws in this state! Policeman and an
ambulance appeared.

"Ruby?" I asked. "Isabel?"

Both were fine. Oh, how glad I was! I noticed a
Yellow Cab right on the corner. "There's a cab right over

46

there on the corner. Please run to catch it and go on to class."
They did. I was grateful to have the proof that they were actually fine.

The policeman spoke to me, "Please get out of the car." His voice was kind.

I was instantly overwhelmed by excruciating pain. My foot! My leg! I could not stand. There was no way I could put weight on my right foot.

As I climbed or was lifted into an ambulance, I told them I wanted to go to the University of Minnesota hospital.

"Wherever she wants to go, I'll go there too," said the California driver of the big white car. He had a white collar around his neck.

I remember nothing after that until I sat up and found myself on a cot in the emergency room at the hospital, my daughter Cathy standing beside me. And then doctors in green coats, and nurses, and riding around and up and down on elevators. An operating room. A doctor appeared who suggested he pull my leg to see if he could straighten something. I screamed. At the sound of my scream and apparent pain, another doctor said, "No, that won't work."

The next thing I knew several doctors at the foot of my bed were having a discussion with my daughter as to what kind of anesthesia they should use. Another anesthetist joined them, and soon even I was included in the conversation. It was finally decided I, because of my age, would not be put to sleep. I would have a spinal. I agreed that that would be my choice.

Toes on my right foot were all broken (or was it only four?). I felt nothing but could hear and see. I remember only voices and the figures of the nurses and doctors. Two arches in the foot were broken. They inserted pins to keep everything straight and together. It was indeed a black tunnel.

The surgery completed, I was in a two-bed room in University Hospital, my right leg imprisoned in a boot that protected a cement-like cast. There were long days and nights—weeks when I learned to know what it's like to be a hospital patient. Good and bad. Bad because I was not in control of Edith's House. Good because I was well cared for—fed, bathed, wheeled up to therapy twice a day, put through the paces with consideration by hard-working physical therapists. When I couldn't sleep and lay wishing I could get up and go to the bathroom, or wishing I could get to sleep, a touch of a button brought a nurse (not always right away!), a kind nurse, usually, with a bed pan or a sleeping pill, or both. Where else would I have so much attention?

Friends visited, sent flowers and cards. I read a little, wrote some letters. I was pleased by all the attention. But all the while I was concerned about the commitments I'd made to speak and read, promoting the sale of the book. I did so want North Star Press to find that the sale of the book would prove to be a good investment for them.

I once remarked when I had been out of the hospital for some time that I never suffered any pain during this time. When Margie Hance heard me say that, she said, "Why then, when I visited you, did you ask the nurse for pain pills?" It's good to know that physical pain does not leave such a train of thought as some other kinds of pain.

I was in the hospital for about four weeks. (I suppose there's a way to check that out, but who cares?) It may have been three weeks when Dr. Lutter ("Hap") came to see me and announced that he had obtained permission to move me to Midway Rehabilitation Center, renowned for its physical therapy department. I spent another four weeks there. It turned out to be strenuous but very beneficial and healing. I do remember well my first days there. I found myself in a huge area, surrounded by aging, aged people, some without legs or maybe one limb missing, all in varying stages of recovery looking like they never could recover. I thought: *I can't believe this. I can't believe I belong here.* Before I left—after I'd lifted pounds and pounds of weights with my legs and my arms, after I'd learned to walk without putting any weight on my right foot and to sit down on a chair with my leg and foot in that cast, after I'd prepared a pretend meal in the pretend kitchen, and after I talked and laughed with these same persons—I could identify with many of them and felt a sense of *belonging*.

Shortly after the surgery, I'd been told that it would be a year before I would be healed enough to walk around Lake Harriet, that I would never again be able to wear the same size shoes on both feet. Hap assured me that the fate originally drawn for me was not going to be that bad. He assured me he'd have me out of the hospital before the end of March. And I was.

But the struggle was not over. Although I could get around, I certainly was unable to navigate stairs, and, so, because the Bruce Avenue house had only one bath, and that on the second floor, the girls and I decided the best place for me would be at Kenwood Isles, where I was, after all, paying rent. They had been busy while I was in the hospital, sorting, moving and reorganizing. They'd moved the essentials to my new condo; I could manage there.

I was sent home with all the apparatus for my recovery—cane, walker, and wheelchair . . . weights to lift, exercise instructions . . . It was not *when* I had planned to move to Kenwood Isles, and it certainly was not how I had hoped to arrive there. But the best laid plans . . .

The good news was that, indeed, a year later, I was walking around the lake, and both shoes were the same size.

On March 23, 1995, I left the hospital and moved to Kenwood Isles. Cathy and Jane and their husbands had much of my furniture (old and new) and many of my personal possessions (many boxes!) waiting for me. Nurses and therapists came to visit me two and three times each week for six weeks. Before long, I was released from my wheelchair, progressed to using a walker and, finally, graduated to a cane. I had aides who drove me to hospital and doctor visits. It was an ordeal, and I was happy to be here but often very impatient. Chalk it all up to experience and part of the long, black tunnel. I was on my way to the light at the end of the tunnel.

One day in May, Dorothy (Ed Settevig's daughter),

phoned with a message from her father. Surely my heart would have missed a beat. What now? He came the next afternoon. After presenting me with a box of candy, he said, "I am now ninety-one years old. When people get this old, they tend to die. I haven't been sleeping very well lately, and I worry that I might die, and there might be something wrong or difficult with my estate, and I think it would be sad—I would feel bad—if something came up and you did not get this condo." He looked around and then came to the point: "So, if you still want to buy this condo, you might pay me $1,000 down today, and I'll sell you the condo."

I agreed to give him a check that day and close the deal on June first after my meeting with Susan and David Graham, who were buying my house, when that sale was finalized.

That was one happy day. I was about healed physically and the owner of this space that I hope will be my home as long as I breathe.

Chapter Seven

Stroke

December, 37 degrees—snow falling

At my typewriter. It's warm but snow is falling, very wet. I want to write this morning. I wish my days were not so crowded. I am in charge of my calendar, but I'm not sure that I do a very good job. Too many days, too crowded. Gigi, president of our Kenwood Isles Homeowners Association, just called trying to schedule a board meeting . . . we'll have the meeting tomorrow. Today I am having my hair cut, lunching with a friend, and (late afternoon) going to the movie two blocks away. Now to write . . .

Now there's a part of me that wants to write about my new life when I moved into this place called Kenwood Isles. But I don't *feel* like writing about this now. The person I really am, the person who lives in this House called Edith, is mind, body, spirit, genes, experience, emotions, and, trusting this Edith, I'm thinking seriously of simply going with the flow . . . and taking time to write about another black tunnel.

When my book *Beginning in Triumph* came out in 1994, Peg Meier of the *Minneapolis Star Tribune* came to my house to interview me. I found it easy to talk with her. I talked a lot, but one thing I was VERY CAREFUL NOT TO TELL HER was that I had had a stroke. It was something I wanted to keep secret.

Over lunch at D'Amicos one day last week, a friend asked me, "Why do you not want to tell anyone that you have

51

had a stroke? Why is it easier for you to tell someone that you have had a mastectomy than to tell someone that you have had a stroke?"

So I'm sitting here, at my desk, staring out the window. Snow is falling. Dismal. Wet. And I'm remembering the stroke . . .

It was the end of 1993. Paul was dead, and I was alone. I was nearing the end of that long dreary tunnel, the hard journey through the mourning tunnel. I was alone. I would now be wholly responsible for my own life—not that I hadn't always been, but this was different. I was in control, in control of decisions, accountable to no one other than myself. I had no reason for anxieties, nothing I needed to worry about, no one I had to take care of but myself. I was free. I had never known such freedom. I never knew how I hated the word widow until Paul died. The word widow was beginning to take on a new meaning. Yes, it was true, I was truly free. Now I had choices such as I'd never before had.

I began to think about the Elderhostel program, a program designed to provide new learning, new educational experiences for people over fifty-five. Some were local, some were holiday-like trips all over the country. They were meant to attract seniors of all classes and ages who had time, energy, and interest in learning and new experiences. I had friends who'd attended some of the offerings, some even in foreign countries. Now at age eighty, I was free to explore these opportunities. It would mean learning new things, meeting new people, going new places. I realized I'd been looking forward to participating in an Elderhostel for a long time, now the time had come for me to take advantage of the opportunity. I was eighty years old. Better get going before I got too old!

In February 1994 I was off to an Elderhostel in Louisiana with Adele Donchenko, a University colleague. We would be at Nichols University in Thibadoux, Louisiana. We flew to New Orleans and, settled into a very old inn in the French Quarter, enjoyed the high spirits of the pre-Mardi Gras festivities, and then drove on to Nichols University.

Housed in dormitories, Adele and I each had our own space. I was in a very large room that held four spare and empty cots. All this space seemed not lonely, but luxurious. We attended lectures on Louisiana history; I'd become fascinated with the strange beauty of the bayou country we'd driven through on our way from New Orleans. Sparsely settled, big skies, the bleak landscape cast a hypnotic charm over me. Every place has its own beauty, and it was fun to hear stories and geographical information about the region. We learned about early inhabitants, how they traveled, how they built their canoes. The days passed quickly, and the week was low key, pleasant, non-stressful.

The morning before our last day, Adele and I were walking across the campus in the middle of the bleak and beautiful bayou country. Adele had a firm hold of my right arm. I felt myself being tugged from my intended path. She brought me to a halt in my walking.

"Edith," she said, "we're turning left to the infirmary. I think you have had a stroke." I was stunned, awe struck, speechless. What was she saying? Me, Edith? I couldn't have a stroke! Was she crazy? "Edith," she continued, "you are slurring your words, and you are not walking in a straight path."

A short time later I was in a wheelchair, being driven through the cold, endless corridors that tie together or separate the mysterious rooms and sections of Nichols University Hospital, to a room where a male doctor talked with me. Adele was at my side. I was grateful for her presence in that time of terrible panic and cold fear. Far from home, in Louisiana, an airplane trip to get home, confusion and a familiar numbness that comes over me when situations happen that are seemingly unreal and impossible. Controlled. No tears, just being for a time, *nothing*. A cardiologist asked me questions. Of course I can't remember them now, so many years later. The doctor asked me to follow his forefinger with my eyes. I couldn't count the number of times I've been through that exercise. He decided I was not in danger, told the two of us to go have lunch, suggested that I take the afternoon off and simply rest.

Off then to the cafeteria where we picked up trays and proceeded to go through the food line. At the end of the line, I reached for a red plastic glass of water.

"Adele," I cried, "my hand doesn't work." I had reached for the red plastic glass (still so vivid in my mind). My mind told my hand to pick up the glass, but my hand would not obey.

There was no question about what to do. Adele marched me right back to the infirmary. In what seemed no time at all I was a registered hospital patient. A beautiful dark-eyed French female cardiologist was now with me. I fell in love with her immediately. (I tend to love doctors, teachers, people I trust to care for me.) She held my hand and told me, "You are trying to have a stroke, but we won't let you."

I was in a room, in a gown, and soon wheeled from place to place for a number of tests. I remember most clearly a Doppler test where I sat close to this small French woman in a somewhat dark room. In front of the two of us was a tank-like fixture in which we viewed my heart. The sound was like a washing machine.

"Notice," she pointed, "there is your heart. See the valves. See the valves open and close just as they are supposed to. It is hard to believe that that is the heart of someone eighty years old." That encouraged me. Maybe this wasn't going to be so awful after all . . .

But it was awful. I was put to bed. They thought this was a T.I.A., a Transitory Ischemic Attack. Not a real stroke but near to a stroke. I was able to call my daughter Cathy in Minneapolis, who called her sister, Jane, in Colorado Springs. I remember thinking it was good Paul did not have to bear this news. I remember that the hospital was noisy, that some people were playing cards out in the hall. Sleep was impossible. Again, I thought about my doctors in Minneapolis, wished—oh, how I wished I were home! My daughters decided that Jane would fly to New Orleans that evening and if possible fly home with me the next day. Sometimes now when I cannot sleep at night I try to remind myself that at least there are no interns or nurses playing cards and laughing loudly outside my door. When I complained to a doctor in the morning, he smiled and told me, "Whoever expects to rest in a hospital will be mistaken. If you want a rest, go to the Holiday Inn, not a hospital."

Jane did fly to New Orleans that evening. It was dark, and she'd been in New Orleans only once before (to run a marathon during which she learned nothing about the geography of the area), but she bravely rented a car, got a map and started driving through the black and rainy night to Thibadoux. I shudder now to remember her drive that night. She became tired, and it was late, and she knew that if she did get to Thibadoux, everything would be closed. Afraid of falling asleep at the wheel, she stopped at a third- or fourth-rate motel. "It didn't matter," she reported later—it would only be for a couple of hours until she could go on. She had an eerie feeling because the place was so very far down the line from even a second-class motel; "There was," she said, "a tattoo parlor and bar attached to the motel." Not trusting the lock on her door, she managed to pile furniture against the door to ensure an undisturbed sleep.

I must have slept sometime for when I woke in the morning, there was Jane sitting beside my bed. I'm sure we both cried. The blessed relief of tears had to be an expression of joy. Joy comes in many colors.

The doctors in Thibadoux called my doctors at the University of Minnesota Hospital, and I was released on the promise that I would go to the emergency room there immediately upon arrival in Minneapolis. This was the very day Adele and I were scheduled to return. I have no recollection of the trip from Thibadoux to New Orleans, but I do remember Adele, Jane, and me riding on a plane together to Minneapolis.

I do have one memory—trying to read *The English Patient*, the book I'd taken to read on the plane. I couldn't make sense of it at all and this makes me laugh as I sit at this typewriter. My brain in such a state! That book! I have since read that book twice; it's one of my favorites. I've seen the film seven times, and the book is on a shelf with my favorite books, books ready to go to that proverbial desert island if the time ever arrives when I may take only three or maybe five books to last me for an indefinite period.

Cathy met us at the airport. We drove, as promised, to Emergency at the University of Minnesota Hospital. I was released and slept in my own bed on Bruce Avenue that night. It was good to have both girls with me. They took me to the hospital in the morning where we had appointments with my regular doctor and a cardiologist. I was placed under the care and supervision of cardiologists and my personal doctors. I have survived.

I see the event, the stroke, as one wide black tunnel. The following weeks were not easy. Jane stayed with me until the cardiologist, Dr. Klassen, and the girls knew I would be all right alone.

This period following the stroke were not days and weeks in which I indulged in heavy journal writing. It always seems strange to me that during my whole life I have found my journal to be a good friend. But there have been some times of great emotional stress when I find myself unable to write. At one time Dr. Klassen and his assistant asked me if I would please write an article about the period following my stroke. Feeling incompetent and unwilling, I refused. Here I am many years later, trying to recall just how it all went.

Both daughters found information and knowledge that turned out to be a comfort and reassurance to me. Such as, it is not uncommon for patients who have a stroke (or an ischematic attack) to be unable to recognize the food on the lower left side of a dinner plate. I found that I could go to the refrigerator to get cottage cheese, and be unable to find it if it had been placed on the lower left side of a shelf. For many weeks, I would clear crumbs from a bread board, and find that I'd left a pile of crumbs on the lower left corner of the board.

Sometimes my mind would get tired and give up . . .

On one memorable Sunday when I'd driven myself to church, I thought I'd lost my keys, and couldn't find one left glove. I drove into the lot where I always parked my car, turned off the engine, got ready to pick up my purse and put on my gloves and go into church. Suddenly I could not find my keys. I looked carefully on the floor of the car, checked the space under the driver's seat and searched through every part of my purse but could not find the keys. I began to panic. I finally got out of the car, was on my knees beside the car, looking quite frantically for the silver gleam that would turn out to be my keys. Nowhere could I find them. A friend who attends my church came over to me and asked, "May I help?"

"I've lost my car keys," I gasped, looking up at him from my kneeling position. Now, this kind man had a wife who had Parkinson's disease. He looked at me and asked, "Have you had any mental problems?" whereupon I breathed with great relief. Bless this kind man! He seemed to understand. After he'd spent some time searching my car and the area I'd been studying around my car, he led me into church. Almost upon entering we met my friend Nancy Baltins who took me by the hand, listened to the problem and found a telephone. I called Cathy, told her the problem. She suggested I go on into the church service. She would bring her set of keys for my car and meet me after church. I suffered through the church service. Cold and scared and frozen without any sense of emotion but panic. For sure now my two wonderful girls would be faced with the problem of getting poor old mother into some nursing home. She was really unable to take care of herself! As I look back now, I can say I don't always forget the bad or hard times because I am right there sitting in the second row on the upper front of Plymouth Church on the bench beside Nancy, Nancy holding my hand . . .

After church, still distressed and perplexed, I found Cathy in the parking lot with her keys. I felt calm just having her there with her comforting arms. She knew I would be all right. I *would* be all right! She suggested I drive my car home.

She would follow. All was well. I drove home, feeling calm and comfortable. This was all routine. I unlocked the back door. The red glove was lying on the table. It had never left home. I'd gone off to church with only one glove. I opened my purse where I'd looked so hard for my keys. There they were, right in my purse. Cathy explained to me . . . . It all seemed clear to her because of what she had read—that my brain had looked so hard for the glove and the glove was not there to be found that it, my brain, simply gave up on looking for the keys. It all seemed clear to her. How was I to trust my mind in the future? That was my fear.

I think it was about six weeks later that Dr. Klassen told me that I was pretty well healed, but that pictures and exams (I don't remember what kind of exams, if he did tell me) revealed that I had actually had a stroke, not merely a transitory ischemic attack. He assured me that I was healed and could go on about my life with no restrictions. He said that, although there were no visible residual effects at all, I would be, for eighteen or more months, in a labile state, that I should not, for instance, even try to balance my check book, that numbers would be a problem. And that is not the end of the story.

It happened again. They said it wasn't a stroke. Only a T.I.A. (Transitory Ischemic Attack). But, yes, traumatic. It occurred in August of the same year, when I flew to Santa Barbara for the wedding of my niece Roxy's son Bryan to Elisa. Only six months after my stroke in Louisiana.

Santa Barbara is a beautiful city. I, with most of the out-of-town guests, was housed in a lovely motel on the shore of the Pacific Ocean. On the day of the wedding, many of us spent the forenoon on the beach. The wedding was scheduled for one or two o'clock. I left the beach to walk back to my motel room, and when I was part way, in the lovely wooded area, I became extremely disorientated and felt lost. I could not figure out how to get to the building where my room was located. I started to panic. (Looking back, I had experienced a similar panic in Louisiana, looking for a confirmation paper early morning of the day I had the stroke. Unreasonable panic in both cases.) Feeling lost like this was terrifying because I'd made this "journey" many times. Before I really went to pieces, I ran into a person I could ask, and went on to my room. It was several hours later after the wedding and during the reception, that I stood on a balcony with my grandson Marc. I turned around to go into the next room, and I found I had no control over my left leg. "Marc!" I cried, "I can't move my leg." A doctor, no more than three or four feet from me, put things in motion, and, in a very short time, I was in a car on my way to Cottage Hospital in Santa Barbara. Doctors, relatives, all these close friends! I could not have been in a better place at a better time. (That's a relative statement!) Cathy flew from Minneapolis. I was well cared for; I survived.

Jane and Cathy.

Edith and Ruth.

Chapter Eight

Christmas, at Age Eighty-five

December 26, 4:00 P.M.—dark cloudy day

At my typewriter, Christmas in the air if not in my head or heart. I am feeling very old today. Have just talked with Margaret U., ninety-six years old, about ten years older than I am, but today I am feeling 110. I am tired and somewhat dispirited. Weather seldom affects me as it does some people, but today I am tired and wishing I had a less crowded calendar. I know there is no one standing beside me telling me what I should do, but I know what I want to get done. Four o'clock in the afternoon is never the best time of day for me. I am a morning person, and it's a slippery slide (What a cliche! It's tough trying to be a writer) in the afternoon. It's actually not so bad to be eighty-five, but when I realize that it's five years less than ninety, I don't like it. Living here with examples such as Margaret who is up on her toes about politics and what's going on in the Middle East, and remembers everything (like history dates) makes me feel insignificant. Politics was never my top interest. How many more Christmases for me? I'm also feeling fat and ugly. Christmas has passed.

∗   ∗   ∗

When I was a child, Christmas was Christmas Eve. Santa Claus and presents and a green pine tree with needles that

61

dropped. My sister and I dripped candle wax on our hands and stuck green pine needles in the wax.

Eighty-five Christmases and now a new Millenium. A new beginning. Like the first robin or falling leaves. Starting school.

Looking forward to this Christmas, I was anticipating no surprises, no unusual happenings. I wanted nothing different. I hoped all would be as usual. Ruthie would come to Minneapolis so we would have some Christmas together. My two grandchildren would be here. I would be with my daughter and her husband. We would have the traditional Hershey Bar Party. The mail, bringing news from old friends, would be fun everyday; there would be a special something in the air. I longed for the usual expectation of wonder and joy. And there were the usual crowds, Christmas carols all over town and on the streets, Salvation Army Santas with buckets and bells, the whole world swinging into a different rhythm: crazy joy, terrible nostalgia, and sadness for many, a heightened sense of awareness, more smiles and conversations with strangers, a coming together of individuals in public places.

The real beginning of this year's Christmas came for me one day in early November when, out from a display in Charlie Orr's Bookstore, I heard a tiny voice whispering to me: "Here I am, Edith, the perfect card for you to send your friends."

The card I held in my hand was a delicate brush stroked painting by a Yurok Indian. Gray and blue blossoms hung from the top and sides of the card. Four small birds flew in a white sky over blue water. The colors and grace of the calligraphy took my breath away as I read:

And now
let us enter
the
Millennium
full of
things that have
never been.

I recognized the echo of Rainer Rilke, the German poet whose lines I quoted for years when writing New Year's letters:

> And now let us believe
> in the new year that is given us,
> new, untouched, full of things
> that have never been.

The brush painting done by Yurok Indians related to a dance as a healing ritual. There was a sense of dance in the painting, an ineffable quality for which there were no words. Poetry came close. I ordered my cards and went on my way. Christmas had begun.

My head was racing with plans for parties coming before Christmas. First would be the dinner in early December for what I call my CEW University Family, five women who worked for me in Continuing Education for Women—a secretary whom I hired and who was with me for the last fifteen years I was on campus, and four women who had worked with us. After that I would look forward to Winter Solstice.

＊　　　　　＊　　　　　＊

I had a good time getting ready for the CEW party. I took the Orrfors crystal ornaments my grandson Scott gave me from their velvet cases, hung them on the chandelier as I have done every Christmas, turned my small round table into a dinner-for-six dining table. Doors to the balcony and the balcony itself were all dressed in garlands of green pine, red-velvet bows and twinkling white lights. I bought new beeswax candles. The table was set with my wedding Spode, purple goblets and stiff napkins. I loved the moment my guests arrived.

Hugs and kisses, greetings of joy from everyone.

"How great you look!"

"I love your new hair do!"

"Isn't it great to be together."

"I'm so glad to see you."

"Isn't it wonderful—no snow this year!"

"You never look any older."

As in the past, everyone brought photographs, told stories, remembered much, filled our wine glasses while we ate hors d'ouvres, and laughed. The pork loin I'd roasted turned out well. We all raved about the vegetables, salads, and desserts the guests brought, feasted on more calories than we knew to be proper for us. The evening was a success. The tradition was alive and well.

I gave three more small dinner parties. Again, everything went well. Nothing went wrong with my cooking. There was good conversation and much laughter. After each evening I was exhausted but fulfilled and satisfied to know I was still able to pull this off. Years ago I used to think giving a dinner party was one of the most fun things in my life—the planning, getting Paul's complete and wonderful support (even if not quite as enthusiastic as my anticipation), having friends around the dining room table. Long ago I would think how much easier it would be if I did not have small children underfoot, and sometimes I would think ". . . if only I had more time."

Now I know that the only thing I need more of is energy. I must be patient and plan well; having no car to hop into and "run to the store to pick up a few things" makes a difference. Not that I have any desire to buy a car and give up the Yellow Cab taxi service. I would miss all my taxi-driving friends and I would miss the luxury of having a taxi at the door every time I ordered one. I would miss feeling as though I were a wealthy woman with a chauffeur who relieves me of the necessary searching for parking places or walking many blocks from a large garage or wondering which door of a building is the proper entrance. And I would miss the money I am saving by not having to care for and fuss about the expenses of a car. The real reason for the success and my happiness with the little dinner parties is that who sits on the chairs is far more important than what is on the table.

*   *   *

No snowstorm, no frigid temperature for the Winter Solstice Party Toni McNaron and Susan Cygnet gave to celebrate Nature's welcome to a new season. A full moon! When clocks reached the hour we were invited to arrive, there was Toni, as was the tradition, waving a flaming torch. We'd been sitting in a car waiting for this moment. Everything just as usual! Just as I hoped it would be. We entered the house lit only by candles. Watching the flames of honest logs burning in the large stone fireplace, we sipped hot spiced tea served in mugs. Each of us brought a candle that will be used for next year's Solstice light. Over the years, we have celebrated beginnings and endings. Every year each woman brings with her a symbol of something that she wants to be rid of, something she wants to be destroyed by the flames, or something she wants to give to the flames that will go out into the whole world. With our gifts to the fire, we share our stories and emotions. It is a sacred time, a holy time. And so it was this year.

The first time I was invited to this party I brought a yardstick that I wanted the fire to burn, to set me free of the *judgmental* attitude that I too often found myself thinking or even worse, expressing. At this most recent Solstice Party, I brought a thick packet of legal sized yellow pages—pages covered with my handwriting in black ink. Paulette Bates Alden, my teacher, friend, and editor, had told me a few months ago, "Edith, I think we have a book here." With such encouragement I had begun seriously to work on what I called "Book in Progress." I was trying not to talk much about this. The few friends in Paulette's writing circle knew I was working on something I was calling *The Eighty-fifth Year*. Now I was sharing it with a wider circle. These women are my friends. I am grateful to be in on this Solstice circle. I had always been overwhelmed by a profound sense of Oneness in this firelit setting—at one with the group and the universe, not alone. This was for my soul. This evening—and full moon thrown in.

*   *   *

The acme of my Christmas may be the annual Hershey Bar Party. I say this because it is the one time during the year that Ruth and I ("The Johnson Girls") gather with our relatives. There is a supposedly humorous cliché about our being able to choose our friends but not our relatives. I have chosen my relatives as some of my best friends.

To begin with, my sister, Ruth, is my best friend. I don't really believe in making judgments (good-better-best) about human relationships. I can't honestly use these terms. All relationships are different. We are, as Aristotle tells us, political animals, and we have many needs, some of which we don't understand at all. I only know that how I feel about my sister, Ruth; I have no words to describe.

We were a small group at the Hershey Bar Party this year. Out of a possible twenty-six people, there were only fourteen of us. Helen Purvey picked me up in her small car; despite the unfamiliar neighborhood and the darkness, Helen found the house easily. Helen is the longtime friend of my grandson Scott. They went to the high school prom together, and Scott is now thirty-nine years old. Christmas lights, white and twinkling, framing it, the house welcomed us. Before I write about this party, it seems only fair that I should introduce my readers to the characters and setting.

Who are these people?

Why is it called the Hershey Bar Party?

How did it start? and what is the history?

*   *   *

I married Paul Mucke. We had two daughters, Cathy and Jane. Ruth married Trygve Runsvold. They had three daughters, Roxanne, Mary, and Beth. Cathy and Roxy were born three weeks apart. Mary and Jane, six weeks apart. Then Ruth had Beth five years later. Roxy married Bill Soth. Alec is their son. It was Alec and his wife, Rachel, who gave this 1999 Hershey Bar Party. Cathy married Bill Hanson, and they had two sons, Scott and Marc. She is now married to Gordon Meagher. Beth is married to Bruce Willis. They have a son, Andrew, and a daughter, Ellen.

Ruth and Tryg moved to Sioux City. For many years, Ruth and I did not spend Christmas together.

People married, were divorced. People died. Babies were born. It must have been over thirty years ago that I first assembled the Johnson Girls' clan for a holiday gathering because Cathy and Roxy are now fifty-nine years old. Our parents gone, Roxy and Cathy were both young mothers, each the mother of two boys, Scott and Marc Hanson, and Bryan and Alec Soth. Roxy and Cathy solved the question of gift giving by giving toddlers Bryan and Scott Hershey bars. The following year when Marc and Alec were no longer infants, they received Hershey bars. And so the little boys started calling the Christmas event the Hershey Bar Party. The name stuck, and the history began. The Soths, Bill and Roxy; Cathy and her husband; the Willises, Bath and Bruce; and I kept the party going. Now, in the third generation, Alec and his wife, Rachel, were giving the party.

That it was their *first* house made it a very special occasion. Now, back to the party . . .

*   *   *

Ruth had arrived with Bill and Roxy Soth before Helen and I arrived. We had no sooner deposited our gifts under the tree and taken off our boots when Cathy and Gordy Meagher arrived with Cathy's son, Scott Hanson. Right after them, the Willis car arrived, with Bruce and Beth, Andrew and Ellen. Now the party could begin.

We explored and praised the house. Down the stairs to look at Alec's gallery, photographs on all the walls. (Alec is the artist in the family—he works for the Minneapolis Institute of Arts). We climbed the stairs to the second floor to check out bedrooms and baths and met the two dogs, properly gated in the guest room. They appeared to be perfectly content even though shut off from the festivities.

The kitchen was cluttered with pots and pans, covered dishes that guests had brought. The tantalizing odor of baking ham filled the air. It made me feel good that the menu was to be as usual.

We feasted on all the usual foods: the honey baked ham, whipped potatoes, whipped cream fruit salad, a hot vegetable casserole, buns and all the condiments to dress up the ham, and Christmas cookies and coffee.

We gathered in a circle as was the usual order of things, expecting the youngest children to pass out the gifts. Although Ellen and Andrew can hardly be called children (Andrew is now in college, and Ellen is thinking about where she will go to college) they agreed to carry on. At the first party I asked everyone to "do something"—sing a song, recite a poem, a personal story. We didn't get any response to that until when very young Andrew and Ellen put on their little shows. One year Andrew performed tricks of magic, Ellen acting as his aide. One year they put on a show, but I can't remember what it was about. One year they did a little dance. We loved everything they did. The mobile lives we lead will bring changes, and who can tell what will happen to the Hershey Bar tradition.

Everyone received presents, hand crafted tree ornaments, books, stationery, Hershey bars, lingerie, gift certificates.

Conversation. Stories. Never the gathering but someone remembers when Bruce and Beth in their new home in Plymouth owned one of the first microwave ovens, and the frozen ham took an unhappily long time to defrost and get hot, or even warm. As I remember, they finally put it in a regular oven.

Everyone remembers the party when Elisa showed up wearing the diamond announcing her engagement to Bryan. Or the party at the Meaghers when Elisa forgot to bring the cake—left it on her own dining room table.

We always remember the Hershey Bar neckties Cathy gave, that turned up year after year, but not last year. I wonder where they are.

Marc, who works for the Hilton Hotel in Reno, told us about the times he was in charge of personnel for House-keeping. One of the male housekeeping boys who cleans and vacuums carpets had a fight with a maid. He stabbed her and left her in a linen closet. She luckily did not die . . . Politics and Governor Ventura had their share of the talk time . . . There was a lot of conversation about computers, how they don't work, what they will do and what they won't do. That talk brought much response from everyone but not from Ruth and me.

I look at Ruth across the room. A waterfall of love gushes through my heart. This hour. This night. I do not have the words. I need a poem. Why does Shakespeare's "parting is such sweet sweet sorrow" come to mind?

She was her usual fashionable self, wearing a white T-shirt under a black jumper with an unusual African design. The skirt was very long. What I saw of her legs was black hose and neat black slippers. She wore gold jewelry and very large gold earrings. How I loved her hearty laughter—just like when she and Mama and I washed and wiped dishes in our Triumph kitchen upstairs over the Store. She is my little sister, the same Ruthie who giggled with me when Sven Peterson, the wall paper hanger, was at our dining room table and said something so funny that we thought we'd "split our sides," and Mama sent us from the table. That little gray-haired old lady across the room is my little sister. Past, present all come together. No time. All time. And I am another little old lady (we have both shrunk to a mere five feet tall). Our four brown eyes have all undergone cataract surgery, never mind that we both now wear platinum framed glasses of an updated design. I wear hearing aids in both ears. She has knee and back problems. I am taking five pills every day. We'd enjoyed these parties for years. She looked happy, sat calmly relaxed, smiling. We looked at each other. All was well with our two families. Was her mind cloud-ed as mine was? Clouded with memories of our two husbands, Tryg and Paul, both dead. The party—anticipated, enjoyed, we were comfortable in the sameness. The Hershey Bar Parties ad infinitum, precious because they are not ad infinitum. And we know it. How long? This hour. This time.

*   *   *

There was never anything profoundly religious about the memories I have of Christmas. My family moved from Minneapolis to Triumph when I was seven years old. We attended a Christian Science Church in Minneapolis. When we moved to Triumph, the closest Christian Science Church was in Fairmont, eighteen miles away. That was too far to drive every Sunday, so Sunday School attendance was not regular.

When Paul and I raised our children, they attended the Christian Science Sunday School. That church does not make a big deal out of the baby Jesus in a manger, shepherds, and angels, so I have little church baggage with which to approach Christmas. I joined Plymouth Congregational Church ten years ago. I attended the Christmas Eve service there for four or five years, but for the last few years I have spent Christmas with my daughter Cathy and her family who live at Lake Minnetonka. I go there on the afternoon of Christmas Eve, spend the night and come home late afternoon Christmas Day. And so it was this year.

I loved being with them. Cathy is organized and creative. Her shopping is finished, presents wrapped, cards mailed before the twenty-fourth. No frantic rushing about. Gordy, her husband, is one of my favorite people. Forget about all those mother-in-law jokes. I believe we like each other a lot. (This is of course my story. I hope I am right). They have no church affiliation, going to church for a wedding or a funeral and I think that's about it.

Childhood memories are, I think, important as to how we look at Christmas, how we feel about Christmas. My childhood memories of Christmas in Triumph do not include any Dickens Cratchet family Christmas party with many children singing and frolicking about. I spent many Christmases embraced in our small family—Papa, Mama, Ruthie, and myself. It was a quiet time. Although there was no formal church involved, we all knew it was a holy time. Papa would not have approved of going to a movie. We often brought Christmas Eve and Christmas Day dinner to "King Oscar," a tall lanky Swede who did odd jobs for Papa in our General Store. King Oscar was a bachelor. But for his occasional bouts with liquor, he was genial, fairly intelligent, and we all liked him. He lived in a small house more aptly described as a shack. He kept it clean and neat. It was one of Ruth's and my duties to deliver the dinners our mother made for him. Always Christmas Eve and Christmas Day dinners. I think we enjoyed doing that. We also delivered other good things from our mother's kitchen at Christmas time—coffee cakes, cookies, her homemade *sylta* to other people. It was, we knew, a time to give to those less fortunate than ourselves.

It was quiet in our house. There was music—Red Seal records we played on the Victrola and classical music our parents liked from the Fried-Eismann cabinet radio. We all read—magazines, papers, books. I remember clearly one Christmas Day when I read *Robinson Crusoe* all day, a book I'd received on Christmas Eve. The weather was very cold (that was before all this global warming), a mean wind was howling. I sat with my feet on the nickel plated fender of our hard-coal heater. The small square isinglass windows of the heater were red. It was a time to enjoy warmth, comfort, and, yes, isolation.

Paul and I with our children had many Christmases without many guests around. As long as our parents were alive, they were with us for Christmas Eve and often, Christmas Day. Some place along the years we switched from Swedish meat balls, lutefisk and *sylta* on Christmas Eve and Turkey for Christmas Day, to roast beef on Christmas Eve and no turkey on Christmas Day. Christmas Day became a day of rest and leisure. We read our new books, wrote thank you letters, made New Year's resolutions, went for walks in the cold air and made delicious sandwiches with the left over roast beef. Sometimes friends dropped in.

All of this is to say that my time with the Meaghers was usual, and I loved it. Scott (Cathy's older son) and Helen, his longtime friend, joined us for Christmas Eve. We drank champagne to toast the season, ourselves, and the Loving Universe; ate shrimp, sardines, and cheese appetizers, and then the traditional roast beef dinner. We all cheered Cathy and Gordy, saying that the roast beef was absolutely perfect, exactly the right shade of pink-red. A great pile of presents awaited us under the tree. Cathy always gives everyone several presents, loves buying or making them, loves wrapping them. She usually gives me something I need or want that I did not know I needed and will enjoy. This year she gave me a new sweatshirt and sweat pants, in a lovely shade of cocoa with brilliant red, blue, and orange patches of color, a new atlas, and a sleep shirt with designs and words. (A book lover never goes to bed alone, gazing into the night sky . . . travel and adventure . . . pictures of writers and books.)

Some years ago, Marilyn Alcott, a friend in New York, introduced me to the acronym WICWAB (What Is Christmas Without A Book?). I have made it my own. Now I give WICWAB presents to most of the people on my Christmas present list.

On Christmas morning we drank coffee, watching through the window the birds in the woods: sparrows, chickadees, and brilliant red cardinals.

Brunch at eleven brought Gordy's daughter Jill and her husband Mike with their one-and-one-half-year-old son, Jake. Jake makes Cathy a grandmother and gives me a third great-grandson—albeit a step-great-grandson. How can I be old enough to be a great-grandmother? Jake brought chatter and life to the day. He thought he was talking, and I enjoyed his being the center of attention. We ate eggs scrambled with Philadelphia cream cheese, pork sausages, bacon, toasted English muffins. More presents. Telephone calls with the New York and Colorado families. Cathy and I cleaned up the kitchen, went for a long walk, and then she took me home. Christmas was over.

It was good for me to come home to my own space at Kenwood Isles. During the evening, I listened to Christmas music, wonderful famous choirs on the tube. I lit three candles, sat quietly in the dark and the stillness, happy to know the Loving Universe was taking good care of me and my family. Life is a fragile thing. I was knowing myself as a blessed woman, an old woman to be sure, but a woman blessed.

Chapter Nine

Wellness

January, 2000—a new Millenium
8:41 A.M.—Kenwood Isles
No sun, snow—35⁰, wind chill 15⁰

A new Millenium. A new century. A new year. A new day, and today I am a writer. Snow is falling. White rooftops. I'm skipping water aerobics to write. The snow continues to fall.

For me, a child born in Minneapolis in 1914, now eighty-five years plus old, there is always a certain excitement about waking to a new snowfall, the real beauty of the white winter. Cars covered with snow, the realization of my personal comfort and security. True, I can't and don't look forward to scooping up handfuls of white fluff to throw snowballs—not possible today because this snow is wet, and it will be sloppy and slushy—but I don't have to worry about driving or transportation in this weather. It's all right to be "retired." And it's all right to be "retiring," quietly looking out my windows. Which of course is not what I'm doing. I'm being a writer today. Maybe looking out the window is the same thing as being a writer. I'm listening to what's going on in my mind. Mindfulness.

My mind turns to the question a friend from Cleveland asked me last night on the telephone.

"But are you *well*, Edith? Really well? How is your health?" Jackie Edelman is a longtime, close friend. Jewish, bright. Good reader. She used to work for us in CEW (Continuing Education for Women). I love Jackie. Jackie's conversations, face to face, long-distance telephone calls, or in the letters she seldom writes, are always full of questions—Why? How? Tell me! It's fun for me to talk with and write to her.

I told her that *almost* every morning I wake, feeling fine—sometimes in response to the non-electric alarm clock beside my bed, on the best days because I am completely slept out, neither needing nor wanting to turn over and close my eyes, but wanting to stretch and stand and move about and, of course, go to the bathroom. Most days I literally stand, raise my arms to the ceiling or the sky and announce to myself, I DON'T HURT. Nothing on or within this envelope of skin HURTS.

Jackie asked me to write to her and tell her my secrets to wellness. I assured her that I had no secrets, no answers, but I promised to write and share with her some of what I've found useful through the years. That makes me notice that now, this morning, in my eighty-fifth year, I check my left knee. Is this arthritis? It's been speaking to me lately. I know that everyone "over a certain age" has one or more of the many different kinds of arthritis. It doesn't bother me much but there are some aches and pains now and then—when I walk too fast, too far, or too long.

I decide to forget the letter to Jackie and my journal for the time being, and do my half hour of meditation and self-practice of Jin Shin Jyutsu. A few years earlier, after the stroke in Thibadoux, Louisiana, I learned about Jin Shin Jyutsu. I had been at an Elderhostel program, and after my stroke, daughter Jane came to Thibadoux to accompany me home and to stay with me. Jane was very interested in Jin Shin Jyutsu and recalled hearing that the practice was effective in the treatment of strokes. She called a friend in Colorado who was able to locate a practitioner in Minneapolis. So Barbara York came into my life.

February. February in Minnesota. Icy cold, mean winds. Lots of snow on the ground. Barbara braved all this weather, found our house, carried her massage table up the long, vertical cement stairs to our front door. It was dark and snowing, nine o'clock at night. Jane and Barbara talked. I listened. And then, a warm blanket wrapped around me, I was on Barbara's table. Her strong loving hands took charge of my body. She touched various parts of my body, pressed, and lightly massaged my body. I thought of this as acupressure. I didn't know anything about acupressure and didn't understand what was going on. I knew only that I was being cared for, beginning to feel less confused, less scared. Tranquility. I began to think, "I will be all right. I will be whole again."

Barbara came to my home twice a week for several weeks. When I was able to drive my car, I drove to her studio. Meanwhile, my cardiologist and my internist were very pleased with my progress. Both doctors volunteered to give me a prescription for this massage called Jin Shin Jyutsu in the hope that my insurance would okay payment for this work. Both cardiologist and internist felt that this treatment was indubitably having a positive effect in my recovery. Since that time I have been seeing Barbara once a month. It is something I do for myself that I consider to be of prime importance in my well being.

It wasn't until after I'd been seeing Barbara for over a year that I learned the history and began to understand what Jin Shin Jyutsu really is. It is not Chinese; it is not acupressure. Said to predate Buddha and Moses, it was re-discovered in the early 1900s by a Master Jiro Murai, who, after a recovery from a "terminal" illness devoted himself to the revival of the art.

There are two important distinctions between Jin Shin Jyutsu and many other massage and oriental healing modalities to which it is often compared. First of all, it is to be seen as an art, as opposed to a technique. A technique is a mechanical manipulation of the hands. This is a skillful creation. It is the awakening to awareness of complete harmony within the self and the universe. Second, Jin Shin Jyutsu is not a physical manipulation of tissue and uses only minimal pressure. The hands are used as "jumper cables" contacting twenty-six "safety energy points" to redirect or unblock the flow of energy along its pathways. A practitioner of Jin Shin Jyutsu is not the "do-er." He simply assists in the flow of an infinite supply of universal energy. The process does not affect the practitioner's personal supply of energy.

In a typical Jin Shin Jyutsu session, which lasts no more than an hour, the receiver remains clothed and lies face up on a cushioned surface. After "listening" to the energy pulses in the wrists, a practitioner uses a harmonizing sequence of flows appropriate for unblocking particular pathways and restoring the energy along a given pathway. There are many pathways in the body all having their own functions and essence. The practitioner's hands work to clear pathways and unlock some of the "safety energy locks" in the body.

A point I found very interesting is that, in his search for meaning in the Art, Jiro Murai studied in the Imperial Library of Japan, read many books, traveled to holy places and sacred geographical locations. After studying the Bible, the Koran, the Talmud, and the *Kojiki* (*Record of Ancient Things*), he found one basic premise in all religions: The secret is that in every philosophy, every system, every Way, is the commandment to LET GO. It's interesting to me that even the various popular successful Twelve Step programs all have as a basic premise: Let Go. We often hear the words LET GO. LET GOD.

In the beginning, I used to feel there was something magical and mysterious about Jin Shin, and that on days I saw Barbara nothing could or would go wrong. Something wonderful was about to happen. Not only would I be all right, but the world and all about me would be better than ever before. Almost childlike.

Now I always fall into a state of deep physical and mental relaxation. I am aware of nothing but her hands and my feeling of complete freedom. I am giving myself permission to really let go. I am aware of various responses in different parts of my body. A tingling in my toes, a warmth inside my arms, sometimes jumping. Sometimes tears come, and I sob but do not know why. I always feel wonderful when that happens. I can feel my body sinking deeper and deeper into her table, into the floor. A surprising quiver. (I am never aware of a sense of being on another plane of consciousness.) When I get down from the table I am "woozy" but free and loose and happy. Now I expect these positive results and wonder less . . . Now I have a sense of *knowing* that I have been nurtured and am in balance and been given a new sense of strength and peace. All is well. I am in harmony with a Loving Universe.

When I come to Barbara's studio for my monthly Jin Shin session, she asks me if I have any special problems. We talk a few minutes, but what interests me especially is how, when she is working, she seems to find the places where my body needs help. Recently I asked her at the end of a session, "How did you know my arms and legs needed special attention?" She told me she simply listens to my body. She understands. There *is* something to it.

*   *   *

Other paths of wellness have been given to me. In 1997, I worked with a personal trainer at the YWCA located directly next to this Kenwood Isles condominium. Michael became my friend as he put me through the paces—stretching, walking (he taught me how to walk—heel, toe, heal, toe, pelvic muscles pulled tight.) He taught me how, when on the blue rubber mats, to pull my seat close to the wall, turn, walk up the wall. I learned to pretend I was Fred Astair or Gene Kelly and would any moment dance right up the wall and across the ceiling. I learned the pretzel and the cobra positions. I learned to use many of the machines. I lifted weights. I reached a point where Michael and I both felt I could consider myself a graduate.

I learned a lot from Michael and his wife, LaJeune. They invited me to a housewarming party when they bought their first house. This is a connection I treasure—one of many casual (but more than casual) connections we have in our lives—like the boy on the bench, like so many extraordinary cab drivers I've talked with in these five years without a car. The world is full of wonderful, interesting people, people from Somalia and Egypt and Greece and some right next door and in my building.

Now Michael has left the Y and I have settled into stretching, water aerobics and the stationery bicycle. I am telling myself that by walking to market, to the post office, to Walgreen's Drug Store, the lake, I am using about all the energy I have. When I moved into this condo, I watched others walk to the lake. Once free of wheelchair and cane after my car accident, I loved walking around the lake. I simply can't do that three-mile walk anymore and have energy left to do what I want to do the rest of the day.

Energy. It's one in the long series of losses we live through and must learn to accept as part of very old age. I can handle this because I have no choice.

I realized that when I write Jackie, I will tell her about my experiences with Jin Shin Jyutsu, and about my working out. I shall also tell her that I continue the practice of meditation as I have learned it from reading Jon Kabat Zinn, Zen Buddhist author of *Wherever You Go There You Are*, and listening to his tapes—and to the tapes of Bernie Siegel. My body has responded and does respond to what is going on in my mind and my emotions too often for me to doubt the power of silent meditation. Meditation is to me one kind of prayer. My twenty minutes a day, alone in complete silence (insofar as it's possible to ignore sounds like the hum of a refrigerator, traffic, the sound of a garbage truck backing up) is truly precious and therapeutic.

Other times, standing or sitting quietly in the sanctuary of Plymouth church, the same quiet meditation brings me peace as I shut out the external world and listen to what is inside of me—that deep well of wisdom and love, a part of the divine that is given to all of us. The stained-glass windows, the voices of the choir, all the connotations of a church where prayer has filled the atmosphere for generations bring me peace and receptivity, openness.

These are my secrets to wellness.

Chapter Ten

Macular Degeneration

February, 19⁰, Sunshine all day—11:00 p.m.,
now at my typewriter

D ark outside, Halogen lamps in my study, wonderful. Read Anne Fadiman's *Ex Libris Confessions of a Common Reader*. I first looked at this book in a New York City bookstore, didn't buy it there because I like to give Charlie Orr's Bookstore in my own neighborhood (Thirty-first and Hennepin) my book business. Loved reading it because I liked her *When the Spirit Catches You, You Fall Down* so much. That she is the daughter of Clifton Fadiman has a strong pull for me. *Ex Libris* confirms the pull. Anne Fadiman had a childhood different from me and anyone I know. What an education, to sit at her father's dinner table every night! This is something to read and re-read. I laugh and try to remember all the things I can learn. How it makes me run for the dictionary. I put everything aside to read this morning.

And now, so many ends to tie up. My desk looks like it's ready to take off for a trip around the world. (My mother always said, about a neighbor's dining room table, "It looked like it's ready for a trip to Europe.") Before that, I saw my dear dentist, Dr. Jennie Schramm. I never mind going to the dentist. No duties for me while I am there. No telephone to answer, no decisions to make. Just lie back in the chair and let Dr. Schramm do whatever is necessary for my teeth to outlive me.

I wish my cousin Harold who took care of my teeth while he was in Dental School at the University of Minnesota could know modern dentistry. Whenever he got a new hygienist, he would show her the gold crown he put in my mouth while he was in school. It earned him a grade of A, and he was careful to let the new employee know that everything else in my mouth that he had done since, was even better. Now he and his wife, Katy, are both underground. What a privilege, what a gift for me to sit here and remember my cousins and write, making it all real again. Writing like this makes me live everything twice. Now, to write . . .

*   *   *

When I started writing about my long life, I thought I'd crawled through enough long black tunnels. I must have known there might be another before the ashes of this body were under grass. No matter how I leave this plane of existence, there's the matter of my exit. For years I have said, quoting Woody Allen, that I don't mind the idea of dying, but I just don't want to be around when it happens. In other words, I was saying that I would like to simply go to sleep some night, preferably right here in my Kenwood Isles bedroom with the bay window and the night sky visible, and not wake up in the morning. Old age is the time you know it's never too late to change your mind. So I've changed my mind. I think about dying a lot. How, at eighty-five, can I not? Saying good-bye, leaving. That's the hard part. Now I've decided I want to *experience* the dying. And I don't want to be alone. I don't want to be unconscious. I have loved Life and *being* alive. I still do. Dying is a part of life and I don't want to miss the experience. And I don't want to be alone. I want someone to hold my hand. I cherish the conversations and hours I had with my mother the last days of her life. Well, that's enough of that.

Back to the black tunnel. I no longer worry about macular degeneration . . . because I have macular degeneration. Yesterday I called the office of Dr. Leslie Jacobson, opthamologist and longtime friend. I told the nurse I'd seen a white circle on a black-and-white grid. She said they'd get me in that very day and could I come at 1:30. My friend Betsy Fennelly (she's in my Wednesday literature class) with whom I'd planned to see a movie that afternoon, drove me out to keep the appointment. She would do an errand at Southdale Mall and wait for me.

*   *   *

"'That which I have so greatly feared has come upon me.' I think that comes from Job. I saw a white circle on the Amsler grid."

That's what I told Dr. Jacobson when he came into his office where I was waiting. He gave me a puzzled look.

"There are other reasons, other things that might be wrong, some other visual problem that would cause a white spot on the Amsler grid."

I relaxed, realizing that Dr. J. didn't want me to have macular degeneration any more than I did. He knows me as an avid reader and a writer. He knew I'd feared this. Further examination with the mysterious machine, however, and his careful attention and examination of what he saw, confirmed my fears.

But then he talked to me. "Hundred of patients have sat in this chair and listened to this news. Some of them," he said, "cannot accept the news. They keep on insisting they will get a different kind of glasses. There must be something to be done! It is the one case we simply have not found a reason for, an explanation, or a remedy . . . ." as though he were apologizing for the whole medical profession. On a plastic model of the eye, he explained the process to me. I was happy to realize I was not crying and knew I wouldn't, and he went on, "Just remember, you will never be so blind you can't take care of yourself."

Betsy picked me up. There are friends who know when to talk, when not to talk, friends who are sensitive to a particular situation. Betsy is that kind of friend. It was good not to have to rely on taxis for this visit. Although Betsy is younger than I am, she's old enough to know all the proper things to say when it was time to talk. We brought out some laughter by repeating all the phrases we know: Old age is not for sissies . . . I still prefer this to being below ground . . . There are many worse things . . . It's not cancer.

When I came home, feeling numb, I could not stop imagining what it would be like to *not* see. I kept looking at everything carefully as though I might be memorizing what I saw. Could I handle not seeing people's faces? Could I manage having to feel for my dishes in the cupboard? Would I know where in the refrigerator to reach for the cheese? How would I know which side of the milk carton to struggle with the always difficult opening? How would I ever find the right shoes in my closet? Would I have to telephone 512-1111 to know the time of day? I can type with my eyes closed but how would I ever find the errors and the transpositions? I know a quarter has rough edges and a nickel is smooth, but how would I ever know the difference between a five-dollar bill and a twenty-dollar bill? Or which sweater was which in my clothes closet? THIS HAS GOT TO STOP! CALM DOWN, EDITH. That's how my mind was rushing, circling about. Then the phone rang. It was Linda Hathaway.

Linda is one of my closest friends. I have known her only five years. Shortly after I moved into Kenwood Isles, Linda was living in an apartment on the river. I was invited to come with one of her friends to a Fourth of July celebration where, from her balcony on the twelfth floor, we watched fireworks on Nicollet Island. Later Linda discovered that I was born on June 14th, 1914, the very date of her dead mother's birth. She seemed to feel that was a special bond. She'd fallen in love with Kenwood Isles and dreamed of buying a condo here—couldn't wait until her fifty-fifth birthday. (Ownership here is open only to persons fifty-five and over.) Some months before Linda was fifty-five, I alerted her to a condo coming up for sale. It resulted in her buying a condo here two doors down the hall from me, although she couldn't officially move for several months. We think this is a "sign" or one of those things "meant to be."

Linda phoned and asked me to come over to her apartment to see something. I applauded the mirror she had just installed over the kitchen counter. We sat down, she lit many candles, poured me a drink and got a non-alcoholic beer for herself. I was comfortable. It was natural and easy for me to tell her my day's experience. And good for me. She was all sympathy and then it was her turn to talk.

"Edith, you know that one of the five men I work for is an opthamologist. I have heard him talk about patients who have macular degeneration. He has many, and I have heard him say there are five positive things to remember." Then she tells me the five things, and I am amazed that she would know them. They are:

It can be a secret if you choose, no one can see it.
It is not disfiguring.
It never leads to cancer.
You will never be too blind to take care of yourself.
It never causes physical pain.

I went to sleep comforted by all of those things and trying to know that of course I would "handle" whatever happens. What's the choice. The way it is, is the way it is.

The next day I saw my friend Su Phenix. She was at one time a student in one of my journal writing courses, a horticulturist for one her careers. She helped me with the garden on Bruce Avenue and introduced me to Jon Kabat Zinn and the book *Wherever You Go, There You Are*. I am fortunate to have friends the ages of my daughters. So now, I once more confided that I had macular degeneration. Obviously I was not choosing to "keep it a secret" despite its being one of the advantages!

A few days later, Su phoned me to give me a list of ten truths she'd worked with during her successful battle with

cancer. She thought they'd be of some help to me and they
are. She doesn't know any author; her sister gave her the list.
Su and I both thank Anonymous. They are helping me too.
This is a slowly progressive disease and certainly it is possible
I will die without ever having gone blind.

Here then is my list:

Macular degeneration cannot

    cripple love

    shatter hope

    corrode faith

    destroy peace

    kill friendships

    suppress memory

    silence courage

    invade the soul

    steal eternal life

    conquer the spirit.

And maybe I will not go through another black tunnel.

Chapter Eleven

My Spiritual Journey

March, late morning, 11:00 A.M. — mean wind, cold

A typical March day, Papa's birthday on the twentieth, Ruthie's on the fifteenth. Blustery. Sunshine, but a mean wind. Glad I don't have to drive a car today. For every time I miss my car, there are ten times I am grateful I don't have to wonder, decide, worry whether to drive or not drive. Yellow Cab has been very good to me. Within two years of my having moved here, I knew I proved that I spend less money on taxi fare than it would cost me to keep a car. Called 824-4444 last night, and when I came out the front door of my building this morning at 7:30 there was my familiar taxi waiting for me, my friend Art at the wheel. He whisked me over to the Wagenstein building, to the Outpatient Clinic of University Hospital. Every three or four weeks I make this trip because I am on a drug called Coumidan. I am saving time. I could never take care of this duty driving a car. I would have to drive over, park, walk from the garage to the lab, walk back to the garage. Today I was home by 8:30. Actually I feel like a rich lady sitting in the back seat of her car being chauffeured through the busy streets, on the freeway and over the beautiful Mississippi River to 315 Delaware Street.

A friend in Johanna's literature class told me a story I like. She used to live in downtown St. Paul. She moved to Shepard's Road. Now, whenever she takes a taxi to the airport she hands the driver a twenty-dollar bill. "That's too much," says the driver.

"It's not *your* fault I live so close to the airport," she replies. "Keep it." She and I agree there's far too much unfair distribution of wealth in this country. Injustice. We feel good when we can manage a bit of redistribution.

I talked with my sister, Ruth, this morning. We talk often. Impatient and disdainful of modern technology (real reason is I don't understand it—computers or black holes, and much else). I celebrate Papa's life and Ruthie's too. Ruth and I do celebrate Alexander Graham Bell. We call for important messages and, most often, trivial matters—like what are we wearing to church, what we had for dinner, our social activities, movies, books we are reading. We rarely fail to agree that this is a *very good season* of our lives. But now, I've been planning to write about spirituality, my spirituality, and I must get going . . .

*   *   *

I looked at the big sky outside my windows, closed my eyes and waited . . . The scene that came before me was my mother sitting at the foot of a double bed, my sister, Ruth, and I under covers. I don't quite get why we were together in the bed because we each had our own room. The bed was brass, and I think my mother got the three of us together for a daily before-going-to-sleep ritual. I think my mother repeated the prayers for years until Ruth and I simply absorbed them. Mother led us in the Lord's Prayer, the Twenty-third Psalm, and our version of "Now I lay me down to sleep." It went like this:

> Now I lay me down to sleep
> I know that God his child will keep.
> I know that God my Life is nigh
> I live in him and cannot die.
> God is my health, I can't be sick;
> God is my strength unfailing quick.
> God is my All, I know no fear
> Since Life and Truth and Love are here.

And then we always said, "God is here, God is there, God is everywhere." I think I must say that those words I absorbed with my mother's milk.

I was never presented with a picture of a human God, and never in my consciousness did I see God as some old man with long white hair and a beard. I don't think we had any pictures of Jesus in our house. I checked this out with my sister recently, and she confirms that we did not . . . One summer when we were young and lived in Triumph, Ruth and I went to a Lutheran summer school. All I remember about that is that we learned—memorized—the books of the Bible. And I think we saw pictures there of Jesus ascending into heaven in lots of golden light. And probably those pictures of Jesus knocking at a door with a little lamb in his arms.

Our mother was a truly spiritual woman. Surely there was something about my mother's faith and assurance that God could always make everything right if we did our part . . . if we just "knew the Truth." And a part of "knowing the Truth" in Christian Science was declaring that error (anything bad) does not exist. She made it clear that God is not something we can ever see or hear but never mind, God IS ALWAYS HERE, THERE AND EVERYWHERE AND ALWAYS LOVES. That's why it never seemed difficult years later for me to accept the idea that the Divine is here, there and everywhere and *in* everything. In my HEART, in all my veins and arteries, in the blood running all through my body, every cell has its own divine spark. Years later when I read a lot of Isaac Bashevis Singer and Martin Buber, the theory was supported.

I stuck with my Christian Science background until my mother's faith in prayer and a Christian Science practitioner led to her death. She neglected to see a doctor about obvious indications of cancer in a lump and sores in her breast. Her death didn't do much for my faith in Christian Science healing, but I did not lose my faith in God.

Following my return to the university after I'd raised our children, I studied much philosophy and existentialism, read Camus and Sartre and Nietschze, and my doubt and my questions turned me into an agnostic. Never an absolutely non-believer. But nobody could prove anything. All the reasons for my former blind faith faded.

I wish I could say that one bright golden morning I stood on the shore of the Atlantic Ocean and was so stunned by the ecstasy of sunrise and surf, so stunned by the Majestic Allness that I experienced a true epiphany and shouted, "Eureka, God is!" and that there was absolute *knowing* in my soul.

The truth is it did not happen that way. There followed a long, slow evolution and growth. I knew I needed something. I longed for the comfort of my lost faith. I joined the Colonial Church of Edina, a so-called Congregational Church. Well, THAT was not what I wanted or needed. I attended a number of New Age seminars and read a lot of New Age stuff. THAT was not what I wanted. Too many holes there. I listened to Pascal's wager: "It's a better bet to believe in God than to say you don't believe." Now that sounds selfish, but I am talking about *my* journey. Sometime before 1990, I started attending Plymouth Church, joined the church, became a part of Nancy Baltin's spiritual growth group. Now I know with real knowing that God *is*. This is enough to know. Important in my growth I see three words as having great significance:

INTENTION   AFFIRMATION   MEDITATION

I intended, wanted to believe. That means I did not mentally set up a barrage of reasons why I did not, could not, believe, could not really know.

Then affirmation. Affirmations are prayers for me. An insistence that God is here, there and everywhere. Deep within me there is an infinite well of wisdom and Love that God bestowed upon me. Keep up the knowing, affirming. Trust. Trust is faith.

Meditation. That's obeying the psalmist who advises "Be Still and Know." All hours, days, weeks, months. Accept the Presence, the PRESENT, the GOOD.

"If your mind isn't clouded with unnecessary things, this is the Best Season of your Life."

*   *   *

Some people believe in miracles. I live by them. How grateful I am! What joy this is. We have had a miracle in our family. I breathe deeply and try to put it all on paper where it becomes REALLY REAL. Maybe I'll then be able to put it to rest and go on knowing trust and gratitude. There is no end of what my imagination is capable of doing with some bare fact. My mind is like a rushing waterfall. What if? What if? Would I ever have the strength to handle it? What if? Can I get calm enough to rejoice in the Loving Care of a Loving Universe?

— Journal entry, 16 April 1999

  It happened a year ago. Jane and Jim, my daughter and her husband, were driving east to Colorado Springs. Leslie, Jane's daughter, her husband Ali and their nine-month-old baby, Samir, were driving west to Salida to see a T-shirt manufacturer regarding work for Boxe Francaise Sports.

  Leslie and Ali with their baby Samir and fourteen-year-old Alexandre had moved from Paris to Colorado the previous fall. They planned to open a boxing gym, Boxe Francaise Sports, in Colorado Springs. Driving through the curving mountain roads, the used Ford Explorer they'd bought malfunctioned. The car began going faster and faster. Ali, the driver alone in the front seat, shifted gears but nothing happened. He stepped on the brakes. Nothing happened. The steering apparatus did not work. They plunged down a thirty-foot embankment toward the Arkansas River. THEY COULD HAVE BEEN KILLED. THEY COULD HAVE BEEN KILLED. They were not killed. They were cradled, held in the arms of the Loving Universe. God of the Muslims, God of the Christians, Gods of the Jews. It seems to me a true miracle. One God of us all.

  The accident happened on a Wednesday. I did not hear about it until Friday. Early the next morning, Saturday,

I had a profound experience. I was awake at four in the morning, had a hard time not dwelling on the accident. Yet I kept coming back to my own joy and happiness that all is well. I was "slept out" and inserted a Jon Kabat Zinn tape in my tape recorder. Through my study of his book and his meditation tapes I have learned much of the benefits of meditation. The tape to which I refer is a *Body Scan* tape used at the Massachusetts Medical Center. Listening to the tape that night, I found a peaceful relaxation, and my body and mind were letting go, sinking into the mattress of my bed. When the tape finished, I turned on my left side, felt that good sense of knowing. Again "whatever gods there be . . . a Loving Universe. God of the Muslims, God of the Jews, God of the Christians . . . " Our Loving Universe, the Creator had cradled and cushioned Leslie, Ali, and Samir. It was cradling me. And then I felt, knew a tangible feeling of soft warm arms around me. I did honestly feel myself being held in the arms of a physical presence—soft, warm, round, full arms holding me. Male? Female? I don't know. But *comfort*. Imagination? Hallucination? Who knows? It doesn't matter. It was my *knowing*.

This is the best season of my life. For all that has been, thanks; for all that is to be, yes. Praise be to God!

I think the bottom line is my definition of God as Principal, Mind, Spirit, Soul, Life, Truth, Love. Creator. Absolute Power. Energy. Life Force. God is here, there and everywhere. And always, love.

Chapter Twelve

Living Here

April, 59⁰, humidity 70%—at my typewriter

Just out of bed. I am leaving ablutions, clothing, breakfast, and meditation until later. For now, I am just reveling in being home. There is not a morning of my life I do not thank God for my condo on the northwest corner of the second floor of this red-brick building on the corner of Hennepin and West Twenty-eighth Street, Minneapolis, but today more than ever. I am thinking about my coming home last night after my annual three weeks at Hibiscus, a resort on Anastasia Island off the east coast of Florida, just south of St. Augustine. It is always hard to leave the beautiful Florida beaches (white sand like sugar), but when the Yellow Cab delivered me to the front door of Kenwood Isles last night, I was thrilled to be home.

As I entered the lobby, I noticed friends Anna Anderson and Margaret Ueland talking together in front of the row of mailboxes. I greeted them and they welcomed me home. I took the opportunity to tell them they are my models. Margaret is ninety-six and Anna will be one hundred in two months. Anna told me she'd just come in from a walk.

"I sleep too much," she said. "I take a lot of naps, and today I just told myself it would be better for me to go for a walk than take a nap."

I remembered an earlier conversation with Anna, the previous summer I think. I was seated on a bench under the

95

canopy that leads to our entrance. Anna joined me. "People look at me funny when I walk," she explained, "because I walk so funny."

"But why?" I asked. "Here you are walking without a cane and getting along so well. Why do they say that?"

"My doctor told me to walk like this, and I'd be fine without a cane."

"Show me how you walk."

"My doctor told me to walk like this because I'd have better balance."

"Please," I asked, "show me just how you walk and why the doctor said it was okay to walk without a cane."

She rose, placed both feet firmly on the ground, stood straight, and turned both legs outward, pointing the toes of each foot outward, her legs further apart.

I stood, took a stance to show I understood. Sure enough! Of course I too am better balanced like this. And I've gone out into the world demonstrating to my same-aged (as me, not Anna) friends what I learned from ninety-nine-year-old Anna . . .

Margaret, the other of my role models, with whom I was chatting, is a member of the banking, writing, civic leaders in the Twin Cities. She taught many of us at Kenwood Isles a lesson when she used her mind to solve a problem we all might run into. We have safety cords in bathrooms, bedrooms, and one in the living room. Margaret fell one day and could not reach a cord. As she lay there wondering what to do, her eyes (she's legally blind but can see some things vaguely) fell upon a stack of magazines. She remembered how annoyed she often was because they are so slippery. A light went on her mind, and she managed to reach for a *slippery* magazine, got it under her butt and using it as a sled, slid herself over to a cord, pulled it, and voila! Help appeared in the form of one of the desk clerks who helped her stand up. All was well. Margaret is active in the League of Women Voters, sends frequent letters to her Congressmen, and has a busy mind, focused and imaginative. She recently asked a friend to please bring her some cold cream from the drug store. The friend agreed, would be happy to do that errand. "And," suggested Margaret, "please be sure there is no sugar in that cream. I don't want it to attract fruit flies."

After my conversation with Anna and Margaret, I stopped at the desk and told Evelyn (and Vivian who was talking to her) that, yes, I'd had a good vacation but was happy to be back. They both assured me they were happy to have me back. Evelyn was my first acquaintance at Kenwood Isles—she was working the day I first came into the building to see an apartment. She is a gentle ladylike widow who works at the front desk. A former school teacher, she is painstaking in her attention to detail, rules, and regulations. She is always pleasant when we ask her to add to the stacks of Xeroxing that goes on in the universe. She takes care of the bulletin board, and makes posters and notices with delightful designs of flowers and illustrations. She knows when people come and go, who is in the hospital or on a trip, and what is going on. She is discrete and careful.

Evelyn handed me the keys she'd been keeping for me; I adjusted my purse over my shoulder, got my two suitcases (both with wheels) adjusted so they fit my hands and started over to the elevator. I thought, "How much better this is than coming home to a big, cold, empty house." Fran got on the elevator with me. She'd just been getting rid of her trash. We talked about how wonderful it is to simply carry this stuff down to the basement as compared to when we lived in our houses—first getting the trash outside to our garages and then on Sunday nights getting the big garbage cans out to the street. She is one of the first friends I made when I moved in; that day she had just come from coffee at the Co-Bun shop across the street, a coffee shop that has for the past five or seven years won first prize for having the best cinnamon rolls in the Twin Cities. I remember running into Fran at the First Edina Bank when we had both been at Kenwood Isles a very short time. We talked of our transition experience and how strange it was to be changing banks. We'd both been at this Edina Bank for over forty years. We were both misty eyed. We went for walks together, saw a couple of movies together, often had supper at the Moose, a restaurant on the second floor of Calhoun Square, a would-be small mall on the corner of Lake and Hennepin. Over suppers at the Moose, we became acquainted. She spends a good part of her winters in California and is always ready for a cup of coffee.

Fran is part of a circle of five of us that have season tickets to the Jungle Theatre. We have dinner, usually at a Greek restaurant, before the play. It has become a part of my Kenwood Isles "texture of my life," and I love the idea that I am still building traditions, storing more memories. When I moved into Kenwood Isles, I never dreamed that I at eighty would make so many new friends. The people here are my community, my family.

It's a short flight from the first floor to the second floor where I live, but a long walk from the elevator to my apartment door. On the way I pass Linda's, just two doors away from mine. I have a rather new and different relationship with Linda. When she learned that I was born on the very same day, month, and year as her dead mother, that her mother and I once worked in the same office, and when, later, I had something to do with her buying a condo here (she is just barely fifty-five), we developed a pseudo mother / daughter relationship. She makes me feel that I am her age, which is a great gift to me.

Between Linda and me lives Jinny, another of our Jungle Theater Group. She is a member of the spiritual growth class at Plymouth Church that I attend, and thus, I knew her before she moved in. Now, living next door to me, she gives me a ride to and from church every Sunday. Proximity of course plays a role in our friendships, and we often have a drink together before dinner when and if we have both decided to go to our downstairs Terrace Room for dinner— her house or mine. We read many of the same books, and are ready to loan milk or bread or provide other neighborly assistance—pull up a hard-to-reach zipper.

I remember when I was in junior high school (and probably senior high also) lying awake before sleep counting my best friends. Who was my very best friend? Who was number two on the list? And then thinking before each September, who will be my best friend this year? A new best friend every year? Wonderful thing about maturity and age, to have outgrown such concerns. We have many needs and need many different friends. One of the things I like about this community is the size of it. The number of persons living here is not so large that it ever feels like an institution. There's nothing institutional about it. Yet there are enough people so that you have a choice of sociability and privacy. Rarely does anyone knock on my door without phoning me first. I like that. There are not a lot of "shoulds." I never feel that if I invite Betty for a nightcap, that I *should* invite anyone else, or if I invite Linda for dinner, I *should* invite Jinny.

Then, home at last. I dumped my bags and purse on the floor of the entry way, stood looking about, savoring my homecoming. I was tired. There is always travail in travel and for me at eighty-five it's a bit more travail than it used to be. It was good to know I had no obligations and could simply sit down on my sofa and look about. One quick glance in the kitchen and at the plants in the sink. Linda had taken care of them during my absence. The orchid was blooming. I was not hungry and had no desires other than to sit down and be.

My condo is #209 but it's higher than the second floor. (We call the ground floor the Terrace floor, and first floor is above that.) When I sit on the balcony I am in the tree tops of giant pines—well, maybe they aren't really giant pines, but tall pines, home for song birds, not pigeons whose excrement like that of the Canada geese on the lake, is a nuisance.

On the ground floor we have common rooms: lobby, Terrace Dining Room where dinner is served every Tuesday through Friday, a library, a party room, and offices.

My two bedroom, two baths, living/dining area and kitchen give me 1,200 square feet of living space—room enough for my books, my typewriter, places to read and sleep and write, eat and cook, and entertain my friends. When my niece Roxy and I began to plan how I would furnish the space, what I would sell or get rid of from my old house, what I would replace, I told her I'd like to see the basic color be purple, my favorite color. I'm pleased with the final results of our choices. When I moved in, I figured I had enough money to go to Europe once a year. When I had no desire to go overseas this year, I had the fun of having both bathrooms wallpapered, walls and ceilings painted, buying new window shades and lamp shades. My environment has always been important to me, and I feel good about my awareness, interest and, yes, enthusiasm, about my home.

I did nothing but sit there quietly, enjoying my room, being home. I sat on my tapestry-covered couch looking about the room. The purple theme in fabrics, all the light, the bookcase with my much loved books, the Chinese umbrella stand my grandson Marc carried home on a plane from San Francisco. It's so heavy I can barely lift it. A doll costumed in red and white—copy of an African dignitary bedecked with gold and brass chains and amulets, a brass bell in one hand, a wooden stick in the other, and a fur hat. My granddaughter Jill sent me this from East Africa. I am passionate about my home here.

I am passionate about Kenwood Isles. From the carpeting in the lobby and the weight of the windows (tall and wide and sometimes difficult to open), to the enigmatic quality of the food served in the dining room (as frenetic as the dispositions of chefs), I am passionate about Kenwood Isles. I belong here. It is the center of my own special place on this globe called Earth.

*　　　　*　　　　*

Kenwood Isles has the three most important characteristics of any home: location, location, location. A two-block walk takes me to Lake of the Isles and a three-mile walk around the lake. (Due to lowering energy, I have now given up an all-the-way-around-the-lake walk.) A two-block walk in another direction takes me to Lund's Market, a pristine super market that is the envy of out of town guests who visit me. Next door is the YWCA where I swim and once worked with my personal trainer, Michael.

There are 132 condos in the building, 165 residents. Condos are never on the market long, sometimes selling the first day listed. The waiting list is always long. Although there is no medical care available, we do have an "I'm Okay" program that provides a way for residents to have their safety checked twice a day. Those of us who choose to belong are responsible for moving a small plate on our doors that lets a checker walking by know if we are home and okay. My children are happy that, unless they hear otherwise, they know their mother is safe and in place at 9:00 A.M. and 9:00 P.M.

Dinner is served downstairs four times a week. Most of us here are not much into cooking although we do have Guyla Smith and Ruthie Paulson, who actually have dinner parties and entertain as they used to in their houses. Ruthie is gracious, lovely to look at, and I can't imagine her ever acting other than truly "ladylike." She comes from my old neighborhood, but I never knew her until she moved in here.

The community of Kenwood Isles is run by an Owners Association with a board of directors and various committees. Gigi Pilhofer is president of our association and is one of many people in the building who have (and use) computers. Gigi was at one time a booking agent for show people and handled the details for the Minneapolis Aquatennial and the St. Paul Winter Carnival. She now works part time for some booking companies. All on her computer. She also takes charge of our every other Saturday Night movie programs. I have been a helper, taking charge of the free popcorn. Attendance is optional, and the audience varies. It's a great way to enjoy a free Saturday night. Another special events program in Gigi's charge is bus trips to plays, restaurants, shopping malls, and other recreational events. (Not that I consider a shopping mall an "event.")

101

I do not own a computer and don't plan to own one. I am straining my own technological skills when I open cat-sup or wine bottles, use my toaster, or pound a nail into the wall to hang a picture. I am nervous when I have to change the ribbon on this typewriter I've used for over eighteen years. I stand in awe of Gigi and the others who have joined the computer age. Jo Lowry is the real computer expert here. She's a former teacher and writer who became "famous" in the field of education while teaching in Kenwood and, I think, other places. She is brilliant, knowledgeable on any-thing concerning educational theories, literature—all kinds—novels, poetry, history. I love sitting at dinner with her in the Terrace Dining Room. The conversation is always lively and interesting. With Jo's creativity, skill and imagination, she cre-ates cards for birthdays and special occasions that delight and amuse her friends. I am glad I am one of them.

The second or third year I lived here I took a trip to the Pacific Northwest with Lucy Bowren, another resident friend. We flew to Seattle, and "did" the San Juan Islands. I'd never seen a rain forest nor any of that part of the world. We had a fine time and are fast friends. She has a car and often drives herself and me to movies that are not shown in one of our neighborhood theaters. The menus here are all art films, the best films in all of the Twin Cities. It's a very special Sunday when Lucy and I go to a movie at 4:30 or 5:00, have a glass of red wine at Lucia's restaurant on Thirty-first and Hennepin or Teja's on Fiftieth Street. Leaving our neighbor-hood makes it all seem special. Lucy has read and reads more books than anyone I have ever known, works the crosswords every day, is bright, informed and talks a lot.

There are sixteen married couples living here. Two are dedicated Quakers. I have often said I never met a Quaker I didn't like. Jack and Mary Phillips, and George and Elizabeth Watson would never make me change my statement. George and Elizabeth live below me. They are true intellectuals, both having taught at the University of Chicago. Elizabeth is a published author. We have three writers in this stack (a stack is a vertical row of apartments with the same configuration). Catherine Murphy and her husband Jim Taylor live above me. Jim and I are both working on books. I call this the writers' stack.

Jack and Mary are also true intellectuals. Mary is one of my best movie-going friends. (You may begin to see I love movies.) Sometimes Jack joins us. They both taught in the St. Cloud area; Jack was a professor of philosophy at St. John's University. The two of them once put on an education and fun program for the association residents. They titled it "The Joy of Thinking." Mary asked Jack a number of questions about philosophy, and Jack answered them in words that this audience could understand. It led to serious as well as humorous discussion.

There is a lot of talent here and residents are generous about sharing it: Frank Kerr is an architect and also a painter. Annette Garceau worked as the costume designer for the Gutherie theater and has given programs on her work. Gini Corrick is a texture fabric designer, designs and makes many of her own clothes. If she's coming to dinner, someone is apt to ask, "What will Gini wear tonight?" Lorna Hubert who for years served as aid to Mayor Peterson has stories to tell. She loves shopping for clothes and is an expert at finding value at the Clothes Line, the Junior League thrift shop in our neighborhood.

*   *   *

I understand that for a community, this community, to work well, we have to be truly concerned about the maintenance of our environment, inside and outside, that we all have to do our part in facing problems, finding solutions for problems, maintaining good staff relationships. That's why I am willing to serve on the board of directors and two committees. I am grateful for the presidents and committee members who have made this community what is the harmonious place I moved into. We all have a big vested interest here. Eating together in the dining room, riding the elevator up and down stairs, attending joint functions in the community (birthday dinners once a month, the anniversary dinner once a year) I have made many friends. Many others I know as I know some distant relatives. I'm interested in their well being and their contentment. I am passionate about Kenwood Isles.

Chapter Thirteen

The Book

May 7th—70⁰
Dark and rainy, but we'll see "flowers in May"

I'm at my desk again. I like dark, rainy days. Days for reading and writing. I'd like to live as long as I can read and write. (I think about death; does anyone eighty-five years old not think about death?) "As long as I can read and write" seems an acceptable answer to how long would I like to live. I don't think it's mentally healthy to dwell too much on the past, but, oh, how I cherish my memories. I have been considering long black tunnels a good many pages. Now I'd like to think about dreams that come true.

I had a dream. I always wanted to write a book. When other little girls read movie magazines with me and said they'd like to grow up and be movie stars, beautiful and famous and rich, I always said I'd like to write a book. I thought writing a book would be about the best thing ever. (Being a writer would be best of all. I started a novel when I was very young, sitting at a desk my mother painted red and white. The heroine had a romantic name—Consuelo. She lived in a faraway romantic city like Miami or San Diego.)

I retired from the University of Minnesota at the age of sixty-nine. I liked the idea of leaving voluntarily; at seventy I would be forced to retire. Friends asked me what I would do, how would I spend my time. I said I'd really like to write a book, but then silently thought it sounds a bit much, so I

105

also said I'd surely take a class from Johanna Kheim. I'd been scheduling her to teach in the non-credit literature classes through the department of Continuing Education for Women, a department within the Extension Division of the University of Minnesota which I'd been running for years. And I might even take a creative writing course.

I followed through on the literature class. Johanna Kheim, a 1958 refugee from Hungary, was in the Humanities Department, and her Ph.D. work was in comparative literature. Books and reading have always been my top interest. I also knew Paulette Bates Alden, a published writer, who had been teaching creative writing classes for us, and I registered to be a student in her class.

Looking forward to all the leisure time I would now be enjoying, I read eagerly new books in Johanna's "One Hundred Years of German Literature" class and also reread old favorites. What would my whole life have been without all these friends? From Carroll Rankin (author of *Dandelion Cottage*) and David Guterson (*Snow Falling on Cedars*) to Thomas Mann (*Magic Mountain*), authors whose books became my friends. How barren the years would have been without all these writers!

In Paulette's class I completed the weekly writing assignments. I listened to other writers read their work, and best of all, I had a chance to read my own, and they listened. Some years earlier, before retirement, I had obeyed a compulsion to get down in words on paper a description of my Papa's Store (like Maya Angelou, I always thought about it in capital letters). It seemed such an important part of my growing up years. Getting it down in black and white would *actualize* it, prove that it was actually true, make it REALLY REAL. While in the writing class, I pulled those pages from my journal/diary and used it for one of the assignments. I enjoyed polishing it up.

I was over fifty years old when I earned my B.A. degree in humanities. I went directly to graduate school, working in the Department of Continuing Education for

Women first as a graduate student, and then as director until I retired. I'd been on campus a long time, loved the campus life. I was on campus during the 1960s and 1970s. These were interesting and exciting times, and the growth of the work we were doing in Continuing Education for Women was exhilarating. It was hard to leave.

While I was in graduate school, I came to know George Hage, professor of Journalism. He taught a class in Literary Journalism. It was in that class I learned how much fun it was to have people read what I wrote and make honest, serious criticism and judgments. Now and then in my life someone has spoken a sentence to me I never forget. When George Hage told me I was a "natural writer," a "talent not easily taught," I packed it in my mind as one of my most cherished treasures. It feeds my ego and lifts me when I feel down.

The Kheim and Alden classes and the memory of the Literary Journalism class fueled my childhood dream of writing a book. I began seriously to write a memoir—the book, *Beginning in Triumph*, that would eventually be published by North Star Press. It was George Hage who, before his death, gave me the title for the book.

*   *   *

Paul, then retired, and I were home together. It was a good time. I enjoyed learning bridge again, went to my classes, took a water aerobics class at the YWCA, and walked around the lake. But I found a lot of time to write, and when I wrote, I was very serious about it. I know that Paul enjoyed the sound of my typewriter keys when I was in my study and he in his office.

There came a time when I thought I had a finished book. I took all my pages to Kinko's for a big fat book. I even gave each daughter a copy for a present. A friend, Marilyn Alcott, who was on the board of Graywolf Press read it, liked it and sent it to an agent she knew in New York City. He returned it with a three page letter congratulating me on the work, wrote that had he seen this manuscript ten years ago he'd have sold it in a minute, but the time wasn't right for my book at that particular time. His kind words (were they in part due to my age?) encouraged me. I began sending it out. I sent it to small presses in Minnesota—Holy Cow Press, Coffee House Press, Milkweed. Rejection letters came in. I then began sending it far and wide to publishing houses in New York and other names I heard. Rejection letters kept coming in. I shared them with Susan Toth, one of my ardent supporters. I shared them with Mary Rockcastle who had been working with me as an editor and critic. Susan told me I had the finest rejection letters she'd ever seen—far better, she said, than any she received. Paul felt more sorry than I about those letters. He hadn't talked to or listened to as many rejection stories as I had. I began to lose hope and thought about self publishing.

Then I sent a smaller manuscript (it finally got to me, that I'd written too much) to the Minnesota Historical Society. Ann Regan, an editor, wrote me that she liked it a lot (said she identified with me) but it didn't fit the requirements the Historical Society had for publishing, wasn't academic enough. A few years later they changed their requirements, and Ann told me at a book signing party for my friend Barbara Stuhler (The Historical Society has published four of Barbara's books) that had those requirements been changed before my manuscript arrived, they'd probably have taken it.

I decided that I would have to start researching the field to see what self-publishing options I had. I talked to myself and thought the thing to do now was to "let go." Paul had often told me one of my problems was that I had a hard time letting go. I don't know what he was thinking about, nothing to do with the book I am sure. But there must have been some truth in his saying that in my inner self; I think he was right. Anyway, I did let go. I thought about the AA line: Let Go, Let God. I didn't really think God was going to have much to do with this, but I did tell myself to give up, let go. Time passed. Paul died in February of 1990. And then on May 7, 1993, I received a telephone call from St. Cloud.

*   *   *

Here is a copy of my journal entry of May 7, 2000.

> Just today [May 7, 2000], when I was searching for something—(I have a love/ hate relationship for the act of *looking for something*. I may not find what I'm looking for, but I may find something I was looking for recently and couldn't find, or I may "run across" something interesting)—here is what I found. I "ran across" a journal (a Chinese-style journal Tony McNaron gave me) in which the first entry I had written, in very large red letters was: "May 7—BIG DAY." And then in blue script,
>
> > I am so excited my heart is
> > pounding
> > my heart beats so fast
> > my ribs are
> > rattling. North Star
> > Press wants to publish
> > my book. Ann Regan
> > (of the Minnesota Historical Society)
> > tells Corinne Dwyer at North Star Press,
> > "Edith's book is
> > beautifully written and
> > important history and needs to be
> > published and certainly not
> > self-published."
> > Anyway on the phone this morning
> > Corinne tells me they want
> > to and will publish my book.
> > Bless my own letting go.
> > Let go and then it happens
> > Letting go different from giving up,

Giving up different from resignation.
Acceptance from resignation.

Then, more big red letters: I GO FORWARD.

*　　　　　*　　　　　*

The first person I called was Susan Toth. I told her that she was the only person I was telling—oh, yes, and Mary Rock- castle, who had been working with me as a critic and editor. And I would tell Paulette but not "the world." Most people wouldn't learn about my being a real author until the book came out.

"Oh, no, Edith," Susan said. "You must enjoy this period, tell everybody! And don't forget that the making of a book takes at least as much time as the gestation period of a human being, and sometimes longer. And don't forget that it takes a lot of patience."

And it did. Making the book, producing the book, took more than nine months because the editor, Corinne Dwyer, suffered the death of her husband when she was in the middle of her work on the book. She was a wonderful editor, took out what didn't belong, changed the order, ending the book with my best writing. She made of it a more "artful cre- ation."

*　　　　　*　　　　　*

Corinne herself delivered the first copies of the book that I could hold in my hand. She drew the sketch of the white satin pumps on the cover, and with the first book she brought me a framed picture of the cover. Her two daughters were with her that morning. The four of us had lunch at the Green Mill celebrating the book. The book actually "came out" on the day of my eightieth birthday.

That morning Peg Meier came to my house to inter- view me. I had sent a copy to the *Star Tribune*. Peg Meier read it and was asked to do a story on it. At 2:00 in the afternoon, I went to the home of my niece Roxy Soth to celebrate my eightieth birthday and the coming out party of *Beginning in Triumph*. Peg Meier was there with a photographer from the *Star*. Corinne Dwyer was there to sell books. I signed 200 books, and no, I did not get writer's cramp. I enjoyed every single minute of the day.

"Garrison Keillor doesn't sell this many books at a signing," said Peg. Corinne, sitting next to her, replied, "But Garrison Keillor isn't eighty years old."

The book has been a success. It came out in 1994. In 1996 North Star did a second printing. "We don't want it to go out of print," said Corinne.

Chapter Fourteen

Land of Medicine Buddha

*June—68⁰—A "What is so rare as a day in June" day
At my typewriter—2:00 P.M.*

This is truly a "rare as a day in June" day. Quiet. And I am having a quiet day. Late breakfast so no lunch, meaning that I am not groggy but full of energy and good spirits and happy to be here at my machine. On such a day I think of childhood pleasures—riding bikes, swimming, picnics—but none of these greater than what I am feeling today—time to write and remember and feel alive. A monk told me once that our mental attitude is the sole determining factor in whether we are happy or "unwell in the heart." I love that "unwell in the heart." So today I am not "unwell in the heart." So happy to be here at my typewriter. Life is good and it's all right to be an old woman.

*   *   *

How good it is at eighty-five, to know that I am still depositing memories in my mental bank. Three days ago I returned from my second Elderhostel, that unique and creative continuing education program for people over fifty-five. A stroke brought to an early conclusion my first participation in the program. It is not the stroke experience that had prevented my attending another Elderhostel. Rather, I felt that the programs are too much like a bus driver going on a bus tour for a holiday—too much like my earlier career in Continuing

Education. I've always known that if a confluence of companion, subject matter and location happened my way, I would be interested again.

All came together when Margaret Smith suggested I join her in an Elderhostel near Santa Cruz, California. The subject of study was to be Buddhism. Two years previous, I had prayed with Muslims in Tunisia. (My granddaughter Leslie who lived in Paris married an Arab, and Jane and I spent ten days with them and his parents, who live in a small town in Tunisia. Their house is right next door to a mosque.) Then the summer after that I prayed with Catholics on Cape Ann. Why not cover another base?

I met Margaret seven or eight years ago when I joined a spiritual growth group at Plymouth Congregational Church. Margaret is one of the finest, most congenial women I've ever traveled with—well educated, thoughtful and provocative. We find ourselves on the same wave length most of the time. Not that we don't have our differences: Margaret does not touch a drop of alcohol; I habitually enjoy a scotch and water or a glass of wine before dinner. Margaret's body thermostat is set to keep her warm. I always want less heat. Margaret likes three meals a day at approximately the same hour; I stay "full" more than four hours. She likes a bath just before going to bed at night; I prefer a shower, first thing in the morning. The bath preferences worked well when sharing a room, as we did when Margaret and I spent eight happy and rewarding days together in the Land of Medicine Buddha: A Center for Healing and Developing a Good Heart. I had never traveled with her until this trip, but, having traveled to Europe, Asia, and Africa, I have had many traveling companions. I used to say I couldn't imagine traveling with someone who never takes a drink but I changed my tune after traveling with Margaret.

We met (both earlier than scheduled) at the Minneapolis/St. Paul airport. Skies were blue. All was right in our world. The view of the Great Salt Lake from above was a first for both of us. Leaving Salt Lake City, boarding a plane for

San Jose, we were unexpectedly upgraded to first class at the last minute. Margaret gives credit to the straw hat I was wearing. She says my hat made both of us look first class. We shared the pleasure of such luxury, lounging in huge leather seats, enjoying the white tablecloths and gourmet Caesar salad served on trays, while people in the coach where we, based on our tickets, belonged, were eating pretzels. We told ourselves angels were taking care of us.

The Land of Medicine Buddha is a retreat center located about ten miles south of Santa Cruz and a short drive from the Pacific. The closest post office is Soquel, a very small town. The retreat is located on fifty-five acres, much of it redwood forest. The drive to it was mostly uphill, a winding road of truly breath-taking beauty. I had hoped it would be on or closer to the Pacific Ocean but no, we were in hilly forestland.

Descriptions of the winding road that reaches the center warned people coming by automobile not to drive in the dark, that the road was difficult and extremely steep. Margaret and I, sitting in the car Shannon, our chauffeur, so skillfully maneuvered up the hill, were thankful to be passengers and not drivers.

When Shannon delivered us to the entrance of the Land of Medicine Buddha, we pridefully assured each other we'd made the right decision to come a day early while the center was still quiet.

Nestled in a clearing, surrounded by towering pines and giant redwoods, stood a long narrow building with a roof so sloping it turned into an overhang. The building, white with the edges painted a strong red, twinkled with small electric lights. A flagstone path led from the road on which we were parked to the front of the house. Blooming white shrubbery and small pine trees flanked the walk. This was the Gompa, the building in which we would have our meetings, practice Qigong, do meditations. The sound of chimes and gongs filling the air drew my attention to the prayer wheel just to the right of the building. A cylindrically shaped structure about five feet high and two or three feet in diameter rested under a white canopy whose peaked top formed a triangle about six feet wide. Heavy red fringe hung from the edges. It, like the Gompa, boasted twinkling electric lights around the edges.

A red-robed monk walked slowly on the stony path around the wheel. He was barefoot. The effect of the lights, the brilliant red colors set off by white fit exactly my image of what a Buddhist center would look like. We knew at this moment we would never leave the place for excursions or trips away from here. It was so like what we expected, a new world, a Buddhist world.

Registration was simple, and we found our sleeping quarters far better than we'd expected: a fairly large room with two single beds, a dresser, a chest of drawers, a front door and a back door that opened out to a balcony overlooking splendid redwood trees and pines, a lush growth of unfamiliar ferns and greens. I breathed hard, eager to get the feel in my nostrils of this air that was filling my lungs. We came to treasure that private balcony as the week went on, sitting in our two chairs reading our books, talking, or simply being.

We took our first hike that afternoon, stopping often to catch our breath and/or admire fallen logs and wild flowers. We'd read about the poison oak abundant there—had read that it is dangerous and must be avoided. We didn't ever recognize it, but, fortunately, we didn't get curious and touch it at any time. This hill was so steep we stopped often so I could catch my breath. We did not follow the trail to the top. That was something we left for the last day of our stay. On this first day all was mystery and majesty, silent and sacred.

The center is run primarily by volunteer staff. Guests are expected to help out at mealtimes by rinsing their own dishes. There is no maid service for the rooms. We brought our own bath towels, an item that seems simple enough until you start packing your suitcase.

While there, we were to abide by the following precepts:

116

Refrain from killing all life forms (including
    mosquitoes).
Refrain from lying, stealing and sexual misconduct.
Refrain from the use of drugs or alcohol.
There is no smoking allowed on this property. If you
    need to smoke there is an area a short walk off
    the property where you can do so.

These precepts gave us no trouble. I never saw a mosquito. We found rinsing the dishes fun. The function was performed on a pleasant shaded porch just off the dining room. The top half of one wall was open to the wooded area outside. Large aluminum dishpans were filled with hot water and contained long handled scrubbing brushes. There was a pail for the garbage and a tall container for the flatware. We were assured that all the dishes would be re-washed and sterilized in machines before being stacked on our buffet tables for the next meal. Conversation was always lively as we left our tables and came together in this family setting.

Although this retreat was scheduled through Elderhostel, it was not the usual Elderhostel. I consider Margaret, who has attended twenty(!) Elderhostels, a veteran. I think she agreed with me that our time there was more tightly scheduled than is usual in those programs.

Breakfast was 7:30 to 8:30 every morning. Because she likes her oatmeal truly hot, Margaret usually beat me to the dining room. After a time, the stuff was like cement, and I learned to eat granola. There was little variation in our menus. In the morning there was oatmeal, a large bowl of granola, more varieties of milk than I knew existed (with different percentages of milk fat down to skim and up to whole milk, buttermilk, chocolate, Lactaid, and more), oranges, bananas, and (after one guest requested them) prunes, a hot water machine for instant coffee and a wide assortment of teas. We made our own toast. The system was efficient and I think satisfactory to all of us.

Have I said there were twenty-one of us? There were eight married couples, ten men and fifteen women. The eight married couples makes sixteen people, and mathematically I am not coming out right. This is not, however, an arithmetic test and doesn't even involve any money, so let me go on without fretting over that inconsistency. Maybe a couple of people came in late and were not on the original list? Who cares? You get the idea of the mix. The important point is that it was a good mix, a great group—well educated, open minds, and good hearts. I was the oldest person there.

At 9:00 every morning, we were busy removing our shoes, donning soft slippers or brushing off the bottoms of our stockinged feet. No shoes in the Gompa!

The Gompa is the real center of the Land of Medicine Buddha. Upon our arrival we had a partial view of that room, or should I call it a hall? We'd noted all the lights, a circle of people sitting around on cushions—meditating we figured. But this morning at 9:00 was our first experience in the room. It took us only a short time to think of it as simply the GOMPA.

Gompa is a Tibetan word meaning "Place to meditate." At first sight it struck me as a "sort of dancing school room or a gym," but, oh, no, it was much too colorful and brightly lighted, alive with statues and images representing different qualities of mind, all of which Buddhists believe are achievable by all human beings. Every inch of wall space was covered. All around the room were tables or altars, chairs, colorful scrolls, statues. The paintings on the colorful scrolls were usually of meditation deities. Looking at them, meditating upon them, is supposed to remind viewers of the potential of every sentient being (a sentient being is defined as one who has feelings and excludes all plant life) to become fully enlightened. The main altar was a Burmese style Buddha called the Shakyamuni Buddha. "Muni" means sage, and "shakya" refers to the clan of his origin. The "mudra" or hand gesture represents his response during his final meditation when evil forces were trying to stop him from achieving

118

enlightenment. They asked him, "Who is your witness that you have attained these realizations?" Shakyamuni put his hand to the earth and said, "The earth is my witness." And then there was an earthquake! The left hand holds a bowl with nectar, which promises freedom from suffering.

Of the many other Buddhas (statues, photographs and scrolls) represented, most common was the Medicine Buddha, and since this was the Land of Medicine Buddha, it seemed to me the most interesting. This Buddha, while he was "on the path" but not yet a Buddha, made a very strong prayer of dedication. He wanted to have special power to benefit those suffering from mental and physical diseases, during a time when diseases, war, natural disaster, and people with minds completely overwhelmed by delusion, were on the increase. His begging bowl is filled with medicinal nectar, and his right hand holds the stem of an arura plant, a special plant with healing properties. His body radiates light. There were eight Medicine Buddhas of various colors, but the blue lapis was the main one. Neither Margaret nor I spent any significant amount of time seriously contemplating the works or this particular Buddha. Never mind, we were both healthy and well all the time there and left feeling "fit as fiddles."

We practiced Qigong for an hour every morning. Qigong (pronounced Chee-gong) is an ancient health care modality that is a piece of Traditional Chinese Medicine (TCM). TCM is the culmination of 2,000 years of clinical observations and application of exercise, acupuncture, acupressure, and meditation to treat human illness and promote well-being. It is based on a few basic principles that describe the interaction of all natural phenomena. Most basic of these concepts is the theory of yin and yang—a natural tendency for all phenomena to gravitate into pairs of opposites—night and day, heaven and earth, heat and cold, up and down. Certain different parts of the body are seen as having channels that relate to each other. When a person is practicing Qigong, he is using energy within his body and energy outside his body together—gathering energy from the outside to combine with his own energy. My own understanding is shallow.

Back to my learning Qigong at our retreat. Patricia Smith, a sixty-year-old blonde with a dancer's body taught us the gentle physical movements, mindful breathing, and increased awareness that is supposed to activate and harmonize Life Energy. She explained that we are all born with Energy in our bodies and that the universe in which we live is also filled with Energy. She told us that when we practice Qigong, we are gathering Energy (Life Force) from our bodies as well as from outside our bodies—benefiting our bodies and the universe. And she told us her story . . .

She is a registered nurse. While working in that profession she had a serious back injury that resulted in the loss of movement in both legs. She lived seven years a complete invalid, confined to a wheelchair. While in this state, she came to Qigong, learned to stand up, use crutches, and finally, to walk. She returned to work, only to go through three traumatic events: breast cancer surgery, a fall from the top of a truck that resulted in a concussion that put her in hospital again, and an automobile accident in which her car was hit by a driver doing sixty miles an hour. That she survived all this with magic ease and harmony, she credits to her use of Qigong. She has now devoted the last five years to this practice and teaching it to others.

She told us it can be a "tool for life," and indeed, for me it has become a life tool. I will never forget Patricia, and I see her every morning on a video I brought home with me. She is demonstrating the movements she taught us, and as I go through the movements I am grateful for her work.

The movements of Qigong are simple, easy to learn deliberate motions that make and keep me flexible. These stretching/reaching movements, combined with deep breathing, have come to be for me a part of my spiritual nurturing, a moving meditation. I like the following:

A young monk asks his master, "What is God?" The master answers, "God is the breath under the breath."

Despite that story, Qigong is not a religion. People of all religions practice Qigong. The movements and the breathing have a calming effect. When I finish my half-hour routine I do feel that I am "between heaven and earth" and I am "embracing the world." The lotus is a powerful symbol, and, as I go through the routine of the lotus (it is nourished by water and wind), the motions I make cause me to center my mind on these natural phenomena. I raise my arms high and wide to "gather in all the sunshine, moonlight, and dew." I have a comfortable, settled, quite wonderful feeling that I and my body are one with the Universe.

After our hour of Qigong at Land of Medicine Buddha, we used the next hour for Energy Massage for Self and Others: Integration, Stimulation and Regeneration. This was a "clothes on" class during which Scott Taylor taught us how to nurture our bodies and the bodies of others, with healing massage.

Lunch was the big meal of our day. We lived on a vegetarian diet. It was an adventure for Margaret and me to eat so many new combinations of vegetables and starches. Always, we had interesting soups for both lunch and supper—carrot, pumpkin, barley, bean, beet, corn. Also at both meals, the buffet held bowls of crisp young greens and other vegetables from the garden on the property. Bottles of salad dressings lined up like soldiers. The kitchen was open all day for a cup of coffee or tea (make yourself). The kitchen help, largely volunteer—genial, kind, interesting young people. The dining room was a happy lively place, so unlike the silent dining room I'd known at the Catholic retreat.

Following lunch we had an hour break (just like camp!) and then a second practice session of Qigong.

At 3:00 (no time for a nap here) we once more gathered in the Gompa to hear the Venerable Thubten Gyatso, a

Edith is in the middle of the second row.

monk from Australia, talk to and with us about Buddhist Transformative Psychology. We all had a good laugh one day when someone asked him, "Just what is Buddhist Transformative Psychology?" and he replied that he didn't really have a definition. He based much of his talking to us on the theory that modern approaches to health and well being involve manipulating the outer conditions of our lives: modifying our diet, changing our work or living environment, having an operation or taking medicine. While these approaches may be helpful, without stable internal peace, they are ultimately ineffectual. Regardless of the physical condition of ourselves or our environment, our mental attitude is the sole determining factor in whether we are happy or unwell in the heart.

His background was impressive: He'd been a psychologist, then a medical doctor who practiced medicine, and from there had gone on to become a monk. He was witty, wise, funny and handsome too. He gave us some history of Tibetan Buddhism, how and what it is and how it works. It's important to know that it is not considered a religion, never political, but rather a path for living life on this planet. It is an individual path that all persons follow on their journey on this planet. They believe in reincarnation, that if one lives well with compassion and caring and love in this life, one will live better in another form on the next plane of existence. We are all born with karma from a previous life and the philosophy undergirding all is to build good karma. That's a simplistic summary that doesn't do the Venerable Gyatso justice.

After our one free period of the day (always started too late) the 5:15 meditation time with the Ven Namdag always came upon us unawares.

An Australian nun, the Ven Namdag rounded out our faculty. She looked to be about fifty, had been a teacher, was the mother of two grown children, and, with no objection from her husband, had happily taken on the vows of nunnery. We'd noticed her walking about the grounds, slowly and yet with a definite sense of direction. Her dark-red garment was short enough to make her big bare feet conspicuous. We learned that the list of vows a woman must take in order to be a nun is far longer than the list required for a monk. Another story about the role of women in Tibetan Buddhism is illustrated by something one of our classmates read in a book he picked up in the Reliquary. He read that it was written that if a woman lived a most virtuous life and built up a lot of good karma she might be lucky enough to be reborn as a male. Hearing that, Margaret and I were taking a dim view of Tibetan Buddhism! Namdag talked about the importance of silence and meditation. I was disappointed that we did so little meditating. I would have liked guided meditations. Often she read to us from readings of the earliest days or talked in very quiet tones. At one session she read from one of the "absolutely untouched" ancient writings, pages and pages that described in gruesome pictures and language how sinners would suffer in hell. Flashing in my mind were the medieval illustrations (in *Pilgrim's Progress*) and medieval paintings of naked bodies in Hell, writhing in agony, surrounded and being consumed by fire, serpents crawling about, lightning and wind. As a child I'd seen pictures of sinners in hell crying and bodies piled on top of each other. I found it all a bit too much.

Two of the evenings we saw videos—the Dalai Lama on tour was one, and the other, *The Little Buddha*, a film I had seen but enjoyed again.

Our last evening we gathered in the meditation hall again—long lines of tables spread with large white sheets of paper. We were supplied with water colors, watched an art teacher paint a mandala, and were invited to put forth our best creative efforts to paint a mandala. I sloshed paint around like a silly child but couldn't get my heart into it. When, later, the gallery was set up, the exhibition was brilliant and glorious. I was sorry I hadn't put my heart into it. The teacher said my painting was "quite profound." Margaret said what she learned was if she ever had to do it again, she'll simply splash paint around and not try to "create" something.

Margaret and I knew we had given ourselves a great present in deciding to spend an extra day in the Land of Medicine Buddha. The Elderhostel guests left after lunch on Friday, leaving the place to Margaret and me. Volunteers, mostly young people, were busy cleaning, cooking and studying. They took time to show us how to get our own lunch and dinner. Late afternoon we walked up the steep trail we'd hiked the first day. Margaret, having made the trip to the temple at the top of the hill earlier in the week, was my guide. Part way up the hill, we stopped at a small building, administration offices for the Foundation for the Preservation of the Mahayana Tradition. The charming Ven Thubten Gyatso was in the office. After pleasant trivial conversation, we told him we were on our way up to the top of the hill to the Temple.

The trail was a mess, blocked in places by large machines engaged in road construction. Even majestic redwoods had been cut down (nothing on the planet is free from road construction!). And here in this remote place large tractors or machines blocked the road. Much of the trail was squishy red clay. We continued on. In a short time, we were aware of someone behind us. It was Gyatso who joined us for the rest of the walk to the temple.

The Buddhist temple is an imposing structure enclosing a forty-foot Buddha. Roadwork and tree cutting was underway to make room for another temple because the height of this Buddha requires it. The improved road to the Reliquary is needed for the convenience of people wishing to visit the remains of their relatives. The doors were open. Taking off our shoes we entered and walked about marveling at the size of the Buddha towering above us. Our monk friend pointed out a number of significant relics and artifacts. Our time with him in this temple was the highlight of the trip, or so we have been telling each other since we came home. He may be one of the wisest men with whom I have ever talked. I loved the twinkle in his eyes. When we discussed the population problem of the world, he reminded us that he was doing *his* part.

The Venerable Gyatso leaves us. Margaret and I position ourselves on chairs outside the temple. High on this small mountain, our backs to the temple, overlooking giant redwoods, maybe yellow-leafed oaks, mindful of pure air on our skin, we listen to the silence. Mystery and magic. Don't let me overuse those words, but I've had many such moments here—like Eden, only I can't lie around nude—too cold, no apples, no snakes. A Softness. Peace. We look at each other. A sense of Knowing. We gather in the beauty of this world wrapped in the spiritual. *Listen to the silence.*

Chapter Fifiteen

Coda

14 June—11:00 P.M., dark and warm, balcony door open

This birthday, end of the eighty-fifth year. I gave myself a present of time. I made no commitments to be any place at any time. Dinner with my family will be tomorrow night. Tonight Adele and Vera, my longtime Edina friends and university colleagues, took me to dinner. Three celebrations I have had and two more are on my calendar. My friend Tom Hunt stopped in this morning, brought me a present—a book from him and his partner John. It's a first novel, *Ana Imagined*, by Perrin Ireland. It's beautifully written, and it's packaged by Graywolf Press with heavy paper, good type and fine binding. I shall read it during my "reward time" reading time—like when my children napped or when my household duties were done, and I felt "free." My friend Lucy Johnson, my neighbor of thirty-seven years on Bruce Avenue who raised her twins while I raised my first child, paid me a surprise visit. She's eighty-nine and drives her car. Little rocky on her balance but she looks wonderful, stylishly dressed in becoming skirt and blouse.

I have twelve yellow roses on the coffee table, and twelve pink roses on the floor next to my balcony. The rooms of my condo are perfumed with love and remembering. Piles of birthday cards—in the mail and under my door. Life is good. I am content as I think about this past eighty-fifth year.

"We live in a word-built world," philosopher Witt-genstein wrote. I've been thinking and trying to put into words for the past year what it has been like and what it means to live a long time and, in particular, what it means to be eighty-five years old.

Life is not fair. I've known from the beginning I can know only about my own life. We are all born in different places, at different times. We crawl through different tunnels, walk through different gardens, open different gates. The beauty of being human is that we are all individuals. We all have the privilege of interpreting our individual experiences in different ways. I have tried to interpret through my lenses and my memory and my mind, my body and my soul what this means to me. How successful has the integration been? How will what I've written, what I think today, appear to me five years from now? Or, if I live that long, ten years from now? Forecasts, guesses, now suggest that in the future the words "a long life" might mean 125 years. At this moment, that strikes no chord of joy with me!

A few days ago, pushing my four-wheeled grocery cart loaded with sixty-seven dollars worth of groceries the two and a half blocks from Lund's market, a hot sun beat down on me (I couldn't find my hat); my knees hurt. The Anxiety Enemy suggested my left hip wasn't quite comfortable. My breathing labored, I stopped to catch my breath; my legs slowed. The trickle that began to sound like a waterfall became five words: "How long, Lord, how Long?" I guess that's from the King James version of the Holy Bible, words unknown scribes of the New Testament imagined to be the words of Jesus, the so-called Son of God.

Death. A part of life. I think about death. Some people say they "never think about it." Others say, "I refuse to dwell on it." Others say, "When the thought comes, I push it away." I think about it. How can I not think about it? I know I will be cremated, my ashes dumped into an urn to be buried at Serenity Garden in Lakewood Cemetery next to Paul's ashes. I have completed and re-done my living will, seen to its placement in the files of my internist and my cardiologist. I have talked with a minister at my church about final rites to ease the tough days for my daughters. Thinking about not being here multiplies, enhances, increases the effervescent joy I know this moment.

For tonight, I like being alive. I'm keeping all available doors and windows open to whatever makes sense to me. I praise and am grateful for all the external factors. I have known for a long time that I was born lucky. (It rhymes with my name, Mucke.) Born white, in the United States, with good genes. (How do genes relate to karma—something over which we have no control, not a lot, but some?) I am grateful for all the teachers I have known, lessons I have been taught, lessons I have learned. I am overwhelmed with gratitude. Gratitude is the oil that lubricates my joints. I shall light a candle, stand on the balcony and say "Thank you," say good night to the city and wish myself a good year ahead.

Wisdom? Conclusions? What about the future?

I think maybe my impulsive answer to the young man on the bench that "To Forgive" is high on my list of what's most important. And very important to love and never to hurt anybody. Being kind makes me feel good.

The House of Edith is not finished . . .

Here, a touch of fresh paint . . .

. . . there, a nail . . .

About the Author

Edith Mucke, a widow since 1990, lives at Kenwood Isles, a condo in Uptown, East Kenwood Isles Neighborhood, Minneapolis, Minnesota. North Star Press published her first book, *Beginning in Triumph,* in 1994 when Edith was eighty years old. She was on the staff of the University of Minnesota from 1971 to 1983 and served as director of Continuing Education for Women from 1974 to 1983. She is the mother of two married daughters, has four grandchildren and two great-grandchildren. At the time of this publication, Edith is eighty-seven years old.